P9-DBX-896

LEE CANTER'S

SUCCEEDING WITH DIFFICULT STUDENTS™

New Strategies for Reaching Your Most
Challenging Students

By Lee Canter
and Marlene Canter

SENIOR EDITOR
Marcia Shank

CONTRIBUTING EDITOR
Bob Winberry

EDITORIAL STAFF
Jacqui Hook
Patricia Sarka
Kathy Winberry

DESIGN
Wobriar Graphics

COVER DESIGN
The Arcane Corporation

COVER ILLUSTRATION
Bill Nelson

©1993 Lee Canter & Associates
P.O. Box 2113, Santa Monica, CA 90407-2113
800-262-4347 310-395-3221

All rights reserved. No part of this publication may be reproduced, stored in a
retrieval system, or transmitted, in any form or by any means, electronic, mechanical,
photocopying, recording or otherwise, without written permission of the copyright
owners.

Printed in the United States of America
First printing February 1993
97 96 95 94   10 9 8 7 6 5 4 3

Library of Congress Catalog Card Number 93-091364
ISBN 0-939007-52-5

DEDICATION

To Joan McClintic

*For inspiring us
to focus our efforts
on the children who are
so often forgotten.*

Lee and Marlene

CONTENTS

ACKNOWLEDGEMENTS

We have been very fortunate to have worked with so many dedicated and skilled professionals whose contributions have meant so much in the development of this book.

To Joan McClintic, Judy Cooper, Janet Robinson and Vic Schneidman for their professional expertise and constructive feedback throughout this project.

To Kathy Winberry and Barbara Schadlow for their special role in the conceptual development of this program.

To Pat Sarka and Jacqui Hook for the care and dedication they gave in critiquing the final manuscript.

To Tom Winberry for the outstanding book cover design.

A heartfelt thank you to all those teachers who attended our workshops during the developmental phase of this project. Your expertise, your feedback and your dedication to helping children were a constant inspiration.

And most importantly, to Marcia Shank and Bob Winberry, our creative associates, for their invaluable contribution through all phases of this book. Without their collaboration this book would not have been possible.

Santa Monica, California   Lee and Marlene Canter
January 1993

INTRODUCTION

It is often said that teaching today is more difficult than ever before. Because of our unique position in the educational community, we know that statement is true. We also know how hard you are working and how frustrated you frequently feel. We empathize with your struggles.

We also know that tomorrow can be a better day for you and your students. Skills and determination can make it happen.

Succeeding With Difficult Students began as a conversation that took place with one of our consultants following an Assertive Discipline workshop. Knowing that Assertive Discipline effectively reaches 90 to 95% of the students in the classroom, and realizing that it's the remaining 5 to 10% who take up the majority of a teacher's time, our consultant began to focus our conversation on the needs of these 5 to 10%.

We decided then that it was time to direct our efforts toward developing specialized techniques for teaching these students who challenge us each day.

As the conversation ensued, we began to think about how fulfilling it would be to reach out to these students—to build bridges instead of walls. How satisfying it would feel to call a child at night after a particularly trying day and say, "I feel bad about the difficult day we had, and I could see that it wasn't easy for you, either. I want you to be successful in class, and I know things can be better. Tomorrow we're going to start over fresh. We'll work to make things better. How does that sound?"

Building relationships with the very children we tend to keep at a distance is the heart of the *Succeeding With Difficult Students* program.

Lee and I have shared a very fulfilling year working on this project, and we're excited about sharing our ideas and techniques with you. It is our hope that by learning these new skills you will feel better prepared to face your tomorrows in the classroom.

The children you teach are the future of our country. As an educator, you provide for them the most influential relationship they may have outside of their families. It is an honor for us to work side by side with you as we strive to make a difference in education.

by Marlene Canter

REACHING OUT TO DIFFICULT STUDENTS

Reaching Out to Difficult Students

Section One of *Succeeding With Difficult Students* focuses on developing an awareness of the issues involved in dealing with these students, and on building a positive, trusting relationship that will ultimately enable you to implement skills and strategies that will lead to increased teacher confidence and higher student achievement and self-esteem.

Who Are Difficult Students?

It's a scene that's played out repeatedly at the start of a new school year: A teacher receives her class list. She quickly scans the names, nodding as she recognizes a student here or there. Then her eyes stop as she locks onto one name that leaps off the page at her. Her stomach tightens. It's a name that's all-too familiar to every teacher on staff. Her heart sinks as she recalls teacher's-lounge stories of the confrontational, angry, and volatile behavior that has punctuated this student's four previous years at the school.

Suddenly the prospects for the year ahead seem a lot bleaker than they did a few minutes earlier. Anxiety, stress, and even a bit of uneasy fear begin to replace the enthusiasm with which she started the day.

And just as surely as her own expectations diminish, the student's chances for a more positive school experience this year also begin to fade.

Difficult students. You know who they are.

It's Lisa who holds court in your classroom with tough, rude remarks, incessant talking, and a hostile attitude that clearly communicates she couldn't care less about what you say or do or think.

It's Ramon who isn't able to let five minutes pass without jumping out of his seat, making noises, bothering other students or calling attention to himself in one way or another.

And it's Garrett who won't even try to do his work no matter what you say or do.

Difficult students are the students who are continually disruptive, persistently defiant, demanding of attention or unmotivated. They are the students who defy your authority and cause you stress, frustration and anger. Many of these students have severe emotional or behavioral problems. They may have been physically or psychologically abused, or born substance-addicted to alcohol, crack or other drugs. Many of them come from home environments where parents have minimal, if any, influence or control over their behavior.

Difficult students are *not* the students in your class who act up occasionally. They're not the ones who once in awhile may cause you to lose your temper. Difficult students are those who engage in disruptive, off-task behavior with great intensity and frequency.

As one embattled teaching veteran commented, "I know exactly who my difficult students are. They're the ones who on the days they are absent I'm happy."

These kids don't misbehave once a day.

They misbehave *seven* times a day.

In short, they are the students with whom your regular classroom management efforts do not work.

> "I've tried everything I know to help Eric behave in class and do his work, but he just doesn't respond like the other kids. Believe me, I try to catch him being good. I praise him when I see him doing anything at all that's the least bit praiseworthy, but he couldn't care less. I might as well be talking to a wall."

What kinds of problems do difficult students present in the classroom? Put any group of teachers together to brainstorm that question and they will come up with a list of behavioral descriptions that looks like this:

- Intense responses
- Talk back; rude
- Constantly off task
- Physically abusive to teacher
- Provoke peers
- Insult teacher's appearance
- Violent behavior with peers
- Chronically absent

- Highly emotional
- Defiant attitude
- One misbehavior after another
- Verbally abusive to teacher
- Non-stop talking
- Don't care
- Chronically tardy
- "Velcro" student: sticks to the teacher

Couple any one of these behaviors with a high degree of frequency and it becomes clear why difficult students are so significant to you. After all, how many students does it take to stop an entire class from functioning? Just one.

> The disruptive behavior of just one student can stop you from teaching and can stop the other students in your classroom from learning.

Simply put, this means that just one student can keep you from doing your job.

Just one student has the potential power to adversely affect your confidence in your ability as a teacher. *Attempting* to deal with this one student day after day can cause your self-esteem to suffer and leave you feeling overwhelmed, frustrated and burned out.

These students literally can make or break your school year. It doesn't matter if the student is a 60-pound third grader or a six-foot two-inch junior in high school. The outcome is the same: Difficult students keep you from getting your professional needs met.

> Teachers are frustrated because of the increasing number of disruptions difficult students cause during class, and also because these students seem to consistently defy all their best-intentioned efforts to reach them.

As the opening scenario illustrates, a teacher often reacts to difficult students based on past experiences and the student is quickly labeled. Once a student is labeled (hyperactive, Attention Deficit Disorder, or just plain impossible) what are his or her chances of ever being seen as a unique individual with potential for succeeding in school?

Even more critical, once a student is so labeled, it's all too easy to drop responsibility—to feel that the student has too many problems—that there's "nothing I can do."

When nothing works with them, difficult students tend to make you forget the confidence you once had in your ability to positively impact each and every student.

The message of this book is that it doesn't have to be this way.

You <u>can</u> succeed with difficult students.

A twelve-year-old student who had been a chronic behavior problem from kindergarten through fifth grade begins in the sixth grade to take responsibility for her behavior.

A tough secondary student is disruptive in four of his five classes, yet in fourth period science he chooses to stay in his seat, do his work and participate in class discussions.

An unmotivated, uncommunicative eighth grader who wouldn't even begin assignments a few months ago, let alone finish them, now approaches her work with a confidence that speaks of higher self-esteem and greater expectations.

What's the reason for these successes?

In each case the answer is a teacher who was both committed to the success of all of his or her students *and* who had the skills to make that success a reality. These teachers, and many others like them, are making a difference daily in the lives of students who have been ignored, passed along and, finally, written off.

This book offers techniques and approaches that teachers like these are using every day. By learning these skills, you will gain the hope and confidence to not only meet your students' needs, but to meet your own professional needs as well.

Difficult students need more.

Today the chances are good that you'll have one or more difficult students in your classroom, students who will attempt to test you to the limits every day of the school year. In the face of these increasing numbers, it is ironic that most teachers have had minimal training in how to work successfully with students who present such problems. Think about the difficult students in your own classroom for a moment. As you have probably already experienced, these students do not respond to you like your other students do.

Why?

They need more from you.

- Difficult students need a teacher who recognizes that building positive relationships is without question the most important factor in succeeding with difficult students.

- Difficult students need behavior management approaches addressed to their specific, individual needs.

You need more, too.

Frustrating, no-win confrontations with difficult students are not good for you. Your self-esteem is at stake. Think about it. At the end of a bad year with a difficult student how do you feel about yourself as a professional?

On the other hand, when you do reach that child no one has been able to reach before, your self-worth soars. Your pride in your ability as a teacher rises and you feel good about being a teacher.

The goal of this book is two-fold:

For You

As an educator, you are the most valuable resource our society has if future generations are going to grow into strong, capable, knowledgeable and responsible adults. You are far too important to be frustrated, overstressed and burned out—unable to do your job the way you'd like to do it.

Teachers today feel pressure and frustration from a wide range of sources. Some problems you can't do much about. You can't single-handedly correct dysfunctional families, pump increased funds into the schools or reduce the violence that is wracking our cities and affecting our kids.

You can, however, alleviate the stress and frustration that come from trying to deal with the difficult students in your classroom. That's where training, and this book, come in. With training, this is something you *can* do for yourself.

For Students

The second goal of this book is to give you the ability to do what you became a teacher for in the first place—to help all of your students, even the most difficult ones, succeed.

You can't "cure" or change these students, but you can create an environment that will help difficult students achieve. Through proactive strategies that focus on positive relationship building you can teach these students the social skills and self-management skills that will give them a chance to have a more successful school experience, higher self-esteem and increased confidence.

You are capable of having a dramatic impact on the quality of your own life and the lives of your students. The process begins when you make a commitment to take charge—to develop the skills and strategies that will empower you to work successfully with difficult students.

Helping difficult students will be among the greatest professional experiences of your career. You can have pride and confidence in knowing that you've done the best you can and that your students have benefited.

Building Trust

When we talk with teachers about the difficult students in their classes we often pose this question right up front: "Do you feel that your students should listen to you?"

The answer is always a resounding *yes.*

Then we ask, "Why should your students listen to you?"

Again, responses are given without hesitation, and this is what we usually hear:

"Because I have their best interests at heart."

"I was expected to listen in school and I did."

"What I have to say is important and will help them."

"How else can I share the information they need?"

"Because I am someone who should be listened to."

We ask these questions to illustrate a point:

The difficult student does not view you as the positive, caring role model you see yourself as. These students do not trust you, do not like school, and do not believe that behaving in school is in their best interest. School has not been a positive experience for these students, consequently, they don't really care what you say to them or ask of them.

This is a difficult concept for many teachers to accept.

Most teachers genuinely perceive themselves to be caring professionals who deserve to be listened to and deserve to be trusted by their students.

This profile is how we see ourselves—and it's how we instinctively expect our students to see us too, and, for the majority of our students, that perception is correct.

However, perceptions that allow us to work effectively with most of our students simply will not work with difficult students.

Given these mistaken perceptions, how then do we react when some students not only don't listen but ignore our requests, behave defiantly, engage in disruptive behavior, become abusive and generally put down anything we say?

> "Get off my case. I don't have to listen to you."

> "I'm not doin' this work 'cause I don't want to, OK?"

First, we think there's something wrong with the students. There must be. They're not giving us the attention we deserve as teachers. They're not responding like other students do—the way we feel they should be responding.

Next, we take it personally. We're hurt. We wonder what we're doing wrong. After all, nobody likes to have good intentions thrown back in their face.

Finally, after feeling hurt, we become frustrated, upset, and angry. In time we often blame the student for causing the problem in the first place.

> "I've done everything I can to reach Andrew. He just doesn't care."

The problem with these responses is that the focus is on the wrong issue. We're letting our own perceptions obscure the fact that the student is dealing with a very different reality—a reality that doesn't have anything to do with you.

Most students arrive in your classroom with a basic foundation of trust in school, and in teachers in particular. Their parents have supported their efforts and have motivated them to behave and succeed in school. These students have generally had positive experiences with teachers and have received reinforcement and encouragement from both home and school.

Experience has taught these students—the majority of your class—that they can trust you, and trust that what you ask of them is in their best interest. Because they are able to trust, they are able to accept your guidance. If you ask them to do something in class, something that they may not particularly *want* to do (an assignment, a job), they'll comply because a basic trust has been built up.

It isn't likely that these students would turn to you and simply say no.

> The difficult student, on the other hand, comes to the classroom with a perception based upon very different experiences.

Many difficult students come from home environments where the parents themselves had negative school experiences, and where respect for teacher and school has not been communicated. Other students come from homes where the adults in their lives have been unreliable role models, unresponsive, abusive or simply overwhelmed and unable to meet their children's needs for motivation and support.

Whatever the origin, these students enter school with a *deficit* of trust in schools, and in the adults who are there to teach and guide them.

As they begin their school years, these students do not instinctively trust that what their teachers ask of them is at all in their best interest. Therefore, when asked to do something, to cooperate, to become responsible members of the class, their responses are often negative and defiant:

"You can't make me!"

"This work is stupid. I'm not doing it."

"I don't care what you say."

This hostility is both hurtful and anger-provoking. A teacher who started off with the best of intentions toward the student finds himself or herself faced with a constant negative barrage. Consequently, the teacher's frustration grows and his or her confidence and self-esteem drop.

And what happens next? Continued defiant responses from the student tend to provoke defiant, negative responses from the teacher and a downward spiral is set into motion. The student's self-esteem is lowered, making his or her chances for success even dimmer. Trust is never established, and ultimately these students fulfill the negative expectations that seem to have been there for them from the start. They do not do well in school. School continues to be an unpleasant experience.

Look at the diagram on the next page. Let's call the center line the Trust Line. Most students, as they proceed through school, accumulate trust in their teachers and in school. Difficult students, on the other hand, feel more and more distrustful of teachers and school and move *down* from the Trust Line. Refer to this diagram as you read the scenarios about Carlos and Sandy.

For Carlos, as you can see, school has generally been a positive experience. From the first days of kindergarten, through elementary school and on to high school he has received positive support and motivation from home. His parents have let him know that they expect him to listen to his teachers and do his best in school. And they have rewarded his efforts with positive attention and expressed pride in his accomplishments. Likewise, his efforts and attitude have earned him more recognition from school.

Over the years, a pattern of trust has built up. His experience tells him that his teachers and school have his best interests at heart. As a result, Carlos is willing to accept the guidance of his teachers and is motivated to make responsible choices that allow him to continue to succeed at school.

Secondary School — Involved in School Activities

Good Relationships with Peers

Continued Parent Involvement

Middle School — Teacher Encouragement

Good Grades

Elementary School — Parental Motivation and Guidance

Gets Along with Teacher and Students

Begins Kindergarten with Positive Support from Parents

Trust Line — **Carlos**

Sandy — Begins Kindergarten: Negative Parent Attitude Toward School

Behavior Problems in Elementary School

Elementary School — Lack of Motivation

Doesn't Get Along with Peers

Defiant Behavior Toward Teachers

Middle School — Detention

Increased Negativity from Teachers

Poor Grades

Secondary School — Suspensions

Sandy, on the other hand, has had a markedly different experience. She came from a home where respect for teachers and school was not instilled. In fact, her parents generally regarded school with suspicion and negativity. They offered little motivation for Sandy to behave in school, and the resulting behavior problems she brought with her to school quickly led to more negativity from teachers. As failure and negativity compounded, Sandy descended further into the deficit of trust. Disruptive behavior and low grades led to even more trouble at school. And lack of interest or guidance at home led to lack of motivation to make any changes.

As the diagram shows, Sandy is now in high school. But by now she's so far below the Trust Line that turning her around is going to take immense effort and determination.

The further below the Trust Line a student moves, the more effort it will take to turn the situation around.

What does all of this mean to you?

Building trust is your first priority in succeeding with difficult students.

The fact is this: If a student doesn't trust you, doesn't believe that you genuinely care, he or she won't ever be compelled or motivated to cooperate with you or to comply with your requests. When a student doesn't trust you, your behavior management efforts will be doomed to failure—after all, this student won't care about either your praise or your consequences. This is one of the reasons your regular classroom management efforts have not worked with the student.

Trust is the foundation upon which everything you need to accomplish with this student must be built.

How do you build trust?

Moving a Difficult Student Back Up Toward the Trust Line

Building trust with a difficult student will be an ongoing process—one that we will focus on throughout this entire book. As was mentioned, the process must start with you—with a shift in your own perception.

You have to change your perception that all students regard you as a trustworthy human being. With some of your students, you will have to make a conscious effort to build this trust.

Only when you make this shift will you be able to look beyond a student's overt disruptive behaviors and accept the following premise.

> It's the way *I* perceive the student and the way *I* act toward him or her that will put me in the position to make some major changes and help him or her succeed in school.

This premise lies at the heart of succeeding with difficult students.

After all, if you feel a student has such overwhelming problems that there's little or nothing you can do to help anyway, do you have any control on improving the situation? No.

If, however, you know that *your* words and *your* actions can make a difference, you empower yourself to develop a relationship with this student that can literally turn his or her life around. With that empowerment you can begin building trust.

Where do you start?

Get to know your student. Put yourself in your student's shoes and look at the world from his eyes, or from her past experiences, and empathize with where he or she is coming from.

(The following story illustrates how Lee Canter guided a teacher toward this understanding.)

> I asked a third-grade teacher to share her feelings about working with a particularly difficult student in her class. Here's what she said:
>
> "I honestly have tried to work with him, but nothing I do seems to make any difference. Manuel is really hard to take. He's either starting fights with other students or he's stuck like glue right next to me. To tell you the truth, he drives me crazy. One minute clinging, the next minute starting trouble. He has an anger that's really scary sometimes. He doesn't listen when I tell him to go outside with the other kids anymore than when I talk to him about his fighting. It's not just me, either. None of his other teachers have ever been able to do anything with him. I don't like feeling that I'm giving up on him, but he's taking valuable time that should be spent on my other students— students who do want to learn."
>
> As she spoke, I could hear her frustration. It was clear that this teacher cared and was frustrated by her lack of success with the student.
>
> Next, I asked her to take a deep breath, close her eyes and try to put herself in Manuel's situation. I asked her to forget her own feelings and, knowing what she knew about her student, speak as if she were Manuel. How does *he* feel about his life and school?
>
> After a few moments she said:

"I, uh, live with my mother and my baby brother. Our apartment is only one room so we put a mattress on the floor at night to sleep. My brother cries a lot so sometimes I don't sleep much. My mother works and she's gone usually until it's dark. When she's home she has her friends over or else she's taking care of my baby brother. My mother says I get in too much trouble at school and she's mad because the school calls her at work. I try to do better but the teachers don't like me and I guess that's why I've been switched to a lot of different classrooms. The other kids don't like me much either and I get mad at them 'cause they're mean to me."

I asked this teacher what she felt while she was speaking as her student.

"It felt very sad being Manuel," she said. "I really was sorry for him. I could feel his despair and his loneliness, and you know what? He's right about how he sees a lot of things in his life. The teachers at our school don't like him. And his mother is overwhelmed with her own problems. I doubt if Manuel has one person in his life that he feels he can count on. He's so tough to deal with that usually what he gets back is anger. It's hard not to be angry at him."

Above the Trust Line

Put yourself in your student's shoes.

Look past the disruptive behaviors and see the child.

Like Manuel, many difficult students haven't had anyone who has consistently and reliably shown them that they've cared. That's why your first objective in succeeding with difficult students is to do everything you can to start moving these students back up toward the Trust Line, to give them something of value to hang onto, because if these students don't feel that you care either, they will fight you every inch of the way.

Before we parted, Manuel's teacher added the following comment:

"You know, right now I really do empathize with Manuel, and where he's coming from. But that feeling will probably last about five minutes when I'm back in the classroom tomorrow and he starts arguing, fighting and disrupting my class. It's one thing to empathize here, away from the situation. It's different when you're in the middle of it."

She's right. Developing empathy and building trust are not simple undertakings. It takes consistent effort, skill and commitment to build trust with a student who is defiant, disruptive or uncooperative. It will take time, too, but you're going to spend time on this student anyway. Why not spend the time in a way that will be beneficial to both of you.

Moving your student back up toward the Trust Line involves planning. You will need to take specific steps to establish a positive relationship with this student. You will have to develop behavior management strategies that recognize his or her individual needs. And you will have to communicate in a manner that is responsive and caring, yet firm.

And what's in all of this for you? As a student builds trust, he or she will become more receptive to your guidance. Your praise will carry meaning. Your consequences will carry weight. As a result, your behavior management efforts will be far more effective and your teaching day far more productive.

In Chapter 3 as we take an in-depth look at the importance of planning, notice the vital role planning plays in reaching out and building trust with a difficult student.

Proactive vs. Reactive Responses

"I have 30 kids in my class and three of them are disruptive and difficult. I know that these three have tough home lives, and have a lot of problems to deal with. But I can't let that stand in the way of their succeeding.

The point is this: I can't change my students' lives, but I can choose how I respond to them. I can't control what these students will do, but I can control *my* responses to make the situation better for both them and me. If all I'm going to do is yell and get angry I won't get anywhere. The way I see it, that means I need to make sure I *don't* scream and yell. I need to make sure I do something different."

Teachers who are successful in working with difficult students understand that they can't change a child, or wave a magic wand and change the problems the child faces each day. But they do know they can change how *they* respond to the child, and that can make all the difference in the world.

These teachers understand that their usual ways of responding to student behavior are not going to work with difficult students. Therefore they give great consideration to planning their responses. They know that they can't walk into the classroom and wing it with difficult students. They need to *know* what they will do when a student is defiant or confrontational.

Nowhere is the lack of planning more apparent than in a teacher's ineffective responses to student misbehavior.

The following scenario illustrates this point.

> Scene: An eighth-grade class is entering the room at the start of the school day. Pat, a consistent behavior problem, noisily makes her way to her seat, yelling across the room to other students and generally taking over the classroom with her disruptive behavior. The teacher looks up from her desk and calls out to Pat.

> Teacher: (*irritated*) Pat, what's the matter with you? Can't you sit down quietly like everyone else?

> Pat: (*slowly seating herself*) I *am* sitting down, Mrs. Peterson. What's your problem? Give me a break.

> With that comment, Pat immediately turns around to the student behind her and begins talking.

> Teacher: (*frustration mounting*) Pat, turn around <u>now</u> and take your books out. I don't want a day like we had yesterday. Do you understand me?

> Pat: Get off my case. What was wrong yesterday? I did my work. I can't help it if *you* had a bad day.

> Now the attention of the entire class is focused on this exchange.

> Teacher: (*anger building*) Don't speak to me like that, young lady. That backtalking has just earned you detention.

> Pat: Oh yeah? Well that's too bad 'cause I have to go home and take care of my little sister after school.

> Class: (*chorusing*) Oooooooooh!

Teacher: (*voice rising*) The rest of you be quiet, unless you all want detention, too. As for you, Pat, we'll see if you have detention or not. I'm sick and tired of dealing with you every single day. It's not fair to me and it's not fair to the other students.

Pat: (*rolling her eyes*) Right. I'm sure they care if they miss any of this boring class.

Teacher: What did you say?

Pat: I said okay, Mrs. Peterson. (*sarcastically while laughing*)

The entire class joins in the laughter.

Teacher: (*losing her temper*) That's it. I'm not putting up with this one minute longer. You're out of here now. Get to the principal's office.

What happened here?

Faced with a defiant, disruptive student, the teacher responded ineffectively. As a result, she became frustrated, got upset and angry. In short, she reacted emotionally to the situation.

Reactive Teachers

Teachers who are unsuccessful in dealing with difficult students are generally reactive. Their emotional responses, as illustrated in this scene, are counterproductive to motivating students to improve behavior.

Let's look at the consequences of this exchange on everyone involved.

Effect on student:

- By reacting in this manner did the teacher help Pat become one bit more successful in the classroom?
- Was Pat ultimately able to get on task?
- Did Pat learn anything at all about choosing more appropriate behavior or was she simply given another opportunity to further hone her self-destructive behavior?
- Did Pat receive any message at all that this teacher cares and is committed to her well being and success?
- Most important, was any trust built between student and teacher?

The answer to all of these questions is no.

Pat did not benefit in any way from this exchange.

Effect on teacher:

- After losing her temper and becoming involved in a no-win argument with Pat, does the teacher feel good about herself?
- Is her self-esteem boosted?
- Is her stress reduced?
- Does she feel she is succeeding with this student or does she feel the frustration of defeat?

Effect on class:

- Has the rest of the class gained any confidence in their teacher's ability to be in charge of the class?
- Has the teacher demonstrated to the other students that she cares about all of their success?

Reactive teachers share these characteristics:

• Reactive teachers don't plan how to deal with difficult students.

They don't actively recognize that these students are different than other students—that these students will consistently present problems that require *preventive* intervention. Instead, the reactive teacher waits until a problem comes up and reacts to it emotionally and ineffectively.

The teacher in the example knew Pat was a difficult student; she knew that she could expect problems from Pat. Even so, she had no plan for dealing with this student and once again was caught in a situation that resulted in her losing her temper and the student being kicked out of class.

• Reactive teachers personalize students' responses.

As the example further illustrates, the teacher took Pat's remarks personally. When Pat attacked both her and the class, she took the bait and was hurt. Hurt quickly gave way to an escalating, hostile, verbal confrontation with the student.

• Reactive teachers give up on students.

A reactive teacher's lack of success with a difficult student often quickly leads to labeling the student ("She's hyperactive! What can I do?") and then giving up. And what happens when a teacher gives up? In the scene, the teacher sent Pat to the office. A temporary respite, perhaps, but one thing is certain: Pat's going to be back and the problems will continue. When we respond reactively, we either keep kicking the student out of class or, out of frustration, let the student keep doing what he or she wants. Either way, the behavior will get worse. Trust drops even further. Problems remain and your stress increases.

> Reactive responses are counterproductive to everything you want to achieve for yourself and for your student.

Proactive Teachers

Teachers who are successful with difficult students are proactive. Being proactive means *planning* how to respond in an effective manner that is respectful toward the student and recognizes his or her needs as an individual. Proactive teachers accept that responsibility and take the initiative to succeed with students. They look at themselves as the leader in the classroom. They recognize that they must have different expectations and develop different responses to difficult students in order for them to be successful.

We've seen a reactive teacher deal with a difficult student. Now, what does a proactive teacher look like?

Let's replay the opening scene, only this time we'll see the teacher respond to Pat in an effective, proactive manner.

> Scene: An eighth-grade class is entering the room. The teacher is at the door, greeting students individually as they walk into the classroom. From down the hall she hears Pat, a consistent behavior problem, noisily making her way toward the room. As soon as Pat arrives at the door, the teacher speaks to her in a friendly, sincere tone. She lightly touches Pat's shoulder as she speaks.

> Teacher: Pat, that was one incredible basketball game you played yesterday afternoon. You are good!

> Pat: Uh, really.

> Teacher: That last basket was quite a shot. (*pause, smile*) The assignment's on the board, Pat. Why don't you sit down and get a good start on it.

> The teacher walks with Pat to her seat. Pat begins her assignment but soon turns around to her neighbor and starts talking. The teacher, already circulating close by, walks over to her.

Teacher: (*leaning down, speaking quietly*) Pat, the assignment is on the board. Please remember, the direction for independent work is no talking.

Pat: I was just asking Andrea what this question meant.

Teacher: (*quietly*) I understand, Pat. But you need to work on your own. If you have any questions, raise your hand and I'll come over.

Pat: What's the big deal? I *am* trying to get my work done! If you'd just leave me alone I'd be fine. It's a stupid assignment anyway. No one's gonna learn anything from this boring work.

Teacher: Pat, you've chosen to wait one minute after class. Now pick up your pen and get to work.

Pat loudly slams her notebook shut on the desk and crosses her arms across her chest. The rest of the class becomes interested in the exchange and laughs.

Teacher: (*quietly, to Pat*) Pat, come over here with me a minute. (*to the class*) Class, continue with your work.

The teacher takes Pat to the side of the classroom. She positions herself so that Pat's back is to the rest of the students, and she speaks quietly in a low, calm tone.

Teacher: Pat, I care about you, and I care that you do well in school. That's why I'm concerned about the poor choices you are making in this class.

Pat: What choices? I *have* to be here, right?

Teacher: (*calmly*) You have a choice right now, Pat. You can either go back to your seat and do your work or we'll call your mom and talk about this problem.

Pat: Right. You're just gonna leave class and phone my mother. She's gonna love that.

Teacher: *(quietly, calmly)* No, Pat, *we* will call your mother together—at lunchtime. You can explain what the problem is to her.

Pat: I'm not calling anyone.

Teacher: It's your choice to make, Pat.

Pat rolls her eyes and mumbles under her breath. Then, with attitude and bravado, she turns and strolls back to her desk. Once there, however, she opens her notebook and gets back to work.

The teacher ignores the provoking body language and instead focuses on whether or not Pat gets back on task. Once she does, she catches her eye and gives her a subtle nod and a smile.

Who was in control in this scene? This teacher knew she could expect problems from Pat, and she had a plan for dealing with them:

- First of all, by greeting her students at the door she had a built-in opportunity for establishing some rapport with Pat. She took advantage of this opportunity by giving Pat positive recognition. (*Building trust*)

- At the same time, she quietly reminded Pat of what she was to do as soon as she sat down, thereby giving Pat some subtle behavior guidance and increasing the chances of her getting on task.

- Once class began, the teacher circulated, staying close to Pat.

- Throughout the verbal exchanges with Pat, the teacher kept speaking in a low, calm voice. This is often disarming to a difficult student who is accustomed to being yelled at. It also allows the student to save face, decreasing his or her need to escalate the situation.

- When it became necessary, the teacher moved Pat to the side of the room to talk one-to-one. Without an audience, Pat was ultimately able to acquiesce without losing face.

- The teacher emphasized that she cared about Pat and was concerned about her. Still speaking in a controlled, quiet voice, the teacher conveyed genuine care and respect for this student. She still, however, held Pat firmly accountable.

- Pat's options were presented as a choice. Clearly it was up to her what would happen next. Just as clearly, the teacher communicated the message that she's "not going away."

Unlike the reactive teacher, the actions this teacher took with her student were not knee-jerk responses. This teacher had a plan for dealing with Pat. What were the results of this planning?

Effect on student:

- Did Pat receive a message that her teacher cares?

- Was she given guidance in choosing more appropriate behavior?

- Was she able to go back to work without losing face in front of her peers?

- Was she treated with dignity and respect at all times?

- Was trust built up a bit more?

The answer to all of these questions is yes.

Effect on teacher:

- Did the teacher stay in control, meeting both her needs and the needs of the difficult student?

- Was she able to remain calm and keep her own stress level down?

- Did she have the satisfaction of knowing that she handled a difficult situation with confidence, caring and professionalism?

Effect on class:

- Was the rest of the class able to stay on task?

- Were the students given a positive example of a caring teacher who respects and acts in the best interests of all her students?

Here's how a proactive teacher approaches working with a difficult student:

• Proactive teachers have individualized, structured plans of action for difficult students.

Proactive teachers recognize that they can't just wing it with difficult students and expect to be successful. Hoping for the best just won't work with disruptive, confrontational and unmotivated students. Proactive teachers realize that without a clearly thought-out plan of action, it is natural (and perhaps unavoidable) to react to difficult students with frustration and anger. They therefore give time to both planning and evaluating how to respond to the students' behavior. They recognize that if they do not proactively plan how to deal with these students the problems will be perpetuated.

> "Of course it takes time and planning. But you don't have enough time not to plan."

• Proactive teachers recognize that they have a choice in how they respond to a student.

These teachers understand that they are in control of their responses—they are not simply passive victims of an out-of-control child. They understand that a student may engage in behaviors they don't like, but *they* are the ones who choose whether or not a verbal outburst turns into a full-blown confrontation.

> If a student swears at you, you can choose not to react angrily.
>
> If a student defies you, you can choose not to respond defensively.
>
> If a student laughs at you, you can choose not to respond with hurt feelings.

You can choose to respond in a very different manner.

The point is, you do have choices to make. You are the one in control, not the student.

• Proactive teachers build positive relationships with difficult students.

Difficult students are accustomed to teachers giving up on them. That's why building trust is so important with these students—their own expectations are so low. Proactive teachers realize that they must consistently show difficult students that they care, that they are not going to go away and that they are going to do everything in their power to help students succeed—no matter how difficult the problem. They consistently communicate a message of hope and success. Proactive teachers don't focus on a student's label. They focus on the student's behavior.

> "I may not be able to change the causes of my student's behavior problems but I will do everything in my power to help change his behavior while he is in my classroom. I don't care if he has been labeled Attention Deficit Disorder or hyperactive or just plain impossible. In my room I'm going to label him a success story."

33

The key to using proactive or preventive strategies is to anticipate problem behaviors before they occur and to plan to help the student succeed where he or she cannot if left on his or her own.

It is all too easy to fall into the trap of using punitive procedures with difficult students. Unless you begin to use proactive strategies to deflect problem behavior when it first appears, you will constantly end up in confrontational, out-of-control situations that will only further erode the already sparse trust the student has in you and in school.

By being proactive you will be able to improve your success with difficult students. You won't be able to solve all problems but you will be able to improve behavior and sustain that improvement.

> "These kids need to know that I care. And showing that I care means treating them with dignity even when they aren't treating me with dignity. Believe me, that takes skill and planning."

Establishing Positive Relationships with Difficult Students

A battleship was among several ships participating in training maneuvers at sea. One cloudy, dark night a thick fog settled over the fleet, making visibility poor. As the fog thickened and the seas grew heavier, a lookout on the battleship reported, "Captain! Light bearing on the starboard bow!"

"Is it steady or moving astern?" the captain questioned from the bridge.

"Steady, sir. We're on a collision course!"

The captain's response was quick, "Signal that ship: *Advise you change course 20 degrees.*"

"Aye aye, sir!"

Almost immediately a signal flashed back to the battleship through the fog: "*Advise you change course 20 degrees.*"

The captain's eyes narrowed as he called out again, "Signalman, send this message: '*You had better listen to me. I'm a captain. Change course 20 degrees.*'"

Within seconds another signal flashed back: "*I'm a seaman second class. Change course 20 degrees.*"

By now the captain was furious. "Send this message, and fast," he ordered the signalman: '*I'm a battleship. Change course 20 degrees.*'"

Back came the flashing light. "*I'm a lighthouse.*"

The captain changed course.

We've included this classic story for a reason. Many of us respond to our students like the captain responded. Because of our *perceptions* we believe we too should be listened to—that students should do what we say. But like the captain in the story, we too will collide head on with the immovable object (the students) if we maintain our misguided beliefs.

Difficult students are like the lighthouse. They are not going to move just because we demand that they do.

Difficult students *should* listen to you but the reality is that they often won't.

Like the captain in the story, you must be the one to change course. And the most effective course to take is one that enables you to build the trusting relationship needed to get the student motivated to really listen to you.

The only way you can build this relationship is to send this message:

I'm your teacher. I care about you and I'm going to do everything in my power to help you succeed. I'm here for you."

To be effective—to be heard by the student—this message must be delivered in two ways:

First, you must build a bridge to the student. Day by day, step by step, you need to work at developing a relationship that clearly demonstrates that you genuinely care about the student, that you believe in his or her potential and that you can be trusted to have his or her best interests at heart. Building this relationship is an ongoing process that we will begin in this chapter, and will be woven throughout all the strategies addressed in this book.

Second, you must always hold the difficult student accountable for his or her actions just as you would hold any other student accountable. You must demonstrate that you have the same expectations for this student as you do any child in your classroom.

Your ability to reach out to a student while at the same time holding him or her accountable to your expectations is what will result in a positive relationship based on mutual trust and respect.

> Not long ago we spoke with a first-year ninth-grade teacher who was cutting her teeth on a tough, tough class. She knew that a lot of her students came from negligent, difficult backgrounds and with real enthusiasm and concern she had decided to show her students that she cared. She couldn't do enough for them. With parental permission she took the students to movies on weekends. They loved the attention and seemed to like her, but the problem was when school began each Monday the behavior problems were still there. After a few weeks of this she began to feel betrayed, bitter and used.
>
> We asked her what she did when the students misbehaved in class. She told us that she did very little other than ask them over and over again to please follow the rules. "These kids have so much else wrong in their lives they don't need me disciplining them."

That's exactly what they did need, of course:

> An adult who would hold them accountable. An adult who was willing to balance positive interest and concern with specific, consistent expectations.

Reaching out is not enough.

Accountability is not enough.

A positive relationship requires a balance of both.

Let's first look then at some techniques you can begin using right away to reach out to your difficult students—techniques that will help you begin to break the habitual negative behavior patterns of these students. Remember, difficult students don't expect you to reach out to them. They expect what they are used to: anger, negativity and low expectations. When they walk into the classroom, this is exactly what they anticipate. As a result, that's what they're prepared for.

They are accustomed to negative relationships with teachers, and they know exactly how to respond to a negative teacher:

They know how to argue.

They know how to confront.

They know how to annoy.

They don't, however:

- know how to respond to a teacher who reaches out to them by putting effort into a positive relationship.
- know how to respond when a teacher greets them at the door with sincere words of welcome.
- know how to respond when they receive an encouraging phone call at home after a bad day.

You *can* break students' negative behavior patterns. When you choose how you will respond to them, their patterns *will* change. It will take time and planning, but look at it this way: Right now 20% of your students may be taking up 80% of your time. You have a choice. You can spend the time proactively reaching out and working with these students to everyone's benefit—or you can spend the time reactively battling with them, to no one's benefit.

Each of the techniques that follow provides an opportunity to let students know you are there for them.

- Call the student before the school year begins.

- Speak with the parent before school begins.

- Take a Student Interest Inventory.

- Greet students at the door.

- Call the student after a bad day.

- Relate to the student one-to-one.

- Make home visits.

Call the student before school begins.

Once you've received your class list (or as soon as you are able to identify a difficult student in your class) telephone the student at home. Most students have never spoken to a teacher on the phone, particularly in a positive context. Imagine the reaction when you reach out to a difficult student just to say hello, introduce yourself and affirm your positive expectations for the year or semester ahead. It's a great opportunity to begin building a positive relationship with the student.

For an easier conversation, write down questions you'd like to ask or things you want to talk about ("How was your summer?" "What's your favorite sport?"), but be sure to include these points also:

1. Let the student know who you are.

Give the student a sincere welcome. Let him know that you are genuinely looking forward to having him in your class.

> "Roland, my name is Mr. Johnson. I'm going to be your geometry teacher this year. I just wanted to give you a call, say hello, and let you know that I'm looking forward to your being in my class this year."

2. Ask the student for ideas about how the school year could be successful.

You just might hear something that will help you in planning how best to work with this student. He or she has probably never been asked before.

> "Roland, I'd like to hear what you think would make this a good year for you. Any suggestions you'd like to give me?"

3. Listen to what the student has to say.

Difficult students rarely are listened to. This is a good way to demonstrate to a student that you care about what he or she has to say. It's a great trust builder.

4. Indicate your confidence that you and the student will work together to have a good year.

Confidence can be contagious. And for this student, it will probably be a unique experience.

> "Roland, I feel good about the year ahead, and I know that if we work together you can be successful and have a good experience as well."

Don't be surprised (or hurt) if the student doesn't say much during the conversation, or seems less than thrilled that you've called. Keep in mind the objective of the phone call—one step in building a positive relationship—one more brick in building the bridge. The fact that you've made the call in the first place will not be lost on the student. What he or she does or doesn't say to you isn't really important. What you say, and the tone in which you say it, is what is important and what will be remembered.

Speak with the parent before school begins.

Developing a relationship with a difficult student means gaining insight and understanding about the student's parent(s), too. Parents of difficult students, like their children, often don't believe that teachers really care. After all, 90% of the contact they've had with school has probably been negative; thus, they typically view contact with school as a criticism. *"What's wrong now?"*

Reaching out to parents of potentially difficult students at the start of the year gives you an opportunity to build trust with them, too.

It's also an opportunity to take proactive steps to build a relationship with the parent—to convince them that you do care about their child and to get them on your side *before* problems arise during the year.

Include these points in your conversation:

1. Begin with a statement of caring.

> "Mrs. Smith? I'm Sara McConnell. I'm going to be Andrea's teacher this year. I wanted to give you a call before school begins to introduce myself and let you know that I'm looking forward to having Andrea in my class this year. I also want to let you know that it's very important to me that Andrea does well this year—I know it's important to you, too."

2. Get parental input about the student's experiences the previous year. (Assess the parent's reality. What does the parent feel about school. *Listen to the parent.*)

> "How do you feel last year went for Andrea? Is there anything you'd like to share that might help me make this year more successful for her?"

3. Get parental input on what the child needs from you this year.

> "Mrs. Smith, what do you think I can do for Andrea that might help her be more successful?"

4. Emphasize that the student will be most successful if teacher and parent work together.

> "I know that you want Andrea to do well in school, and so do I. The best thing we can do for her is to help her understand that you and I are working together for her success—that we both care and that we both believe that she can be successful."

5. Express your confidence that by working together the child will have a more successful experience at school.

> "I am certain that by working together we can make this year the best ever for Andrea. I'm really excited about the year ahead, and I hope you feel the same way."

If the parent responds negatively to your call, take time to listen—take the time to appreciate where the parent is coming from. Then take the time to sincerely communicate that you really do care about the child—that no matter what has gone on before, you are committed to the child's success now and are prepared to do what it takes to make that success a reality. You may not win the parent over immediately, but, like building a bridge with the student, this call is just the first step of many to come.

Take a Student Interest Inventory.

A Student Interest Inventory, taken at the beginning of the year, is a great way to learn more about all of your students. It's also an especially effective vehicle for gaining insight into the interests of your difficult student(s). This information can be helpful to you as you continue to build a positive relationship with the student.

For example, if you find that a student has an interest in dinosaurs, make him or her the class "expert" in that subject—then design a lesson around it. Give the student an opportunity to shine! If the student loves a particular sport, call upon him or her to "coach" other less-skilled students. If a student enjoys art, ask him or her to create something to decorate the room or to design an invitation or other communication going home.

The point is to use the information you learn to build self-esteem in the student. This is information you might otherwise never have had.

A sample Student Interest Inventory is shown on the following page.

STUDENT INTEREST INVENTORY

Name _____

Adults who live with me:

Name_____

Name_____

Name_____

Name_____

Brothers and Sisters

Name _____ Age_____

Name _____ Age_____

Name _____ Age_____

Name _____ Age_____

Special friends: _____   _____

                       _____   _____

What I like to do most at home: _____

_____

These are my favorite hobbies: _____

_____

This is my favorite book: _____

This is my favorite TV show: _____

This is my favorite movie: _____

If I had one wish, I would want to: _____

_____

School would be better if: _____

_____

If I had a million dollars, I would: _____

_____

This is what my teacher did last year that I liked the most: _____

_____

_____

This is what my teacher did last year that I liked the least: _____

_____

Greet all students at the door.

This technique, demonstrated in the script on page 28, is an extremely easy and effective way to ensure positive contact with all students each day, whatever the grade level. It's especially effective with older, tough students because it doesn't single anyone out, yet allows everyone to receive some positive attention—a high five, a handshake or friendly words. Just station yourself outside the door and wait for students to arrive. One by one, give some positive attention as they enter the room. With difficult students, particularly older ones, these might be the only positive words they hear from an adult all day.

> "When I leave in the morning my dad's usually yelling at me and my little sisters are crying and making a big fuss. Then all the way to school I'll be looking behind me to see who's there, who might be following me. Who's out to get me, you know. It's dangerous in my neighborhood, man. First period I have Mr. Fernandez and you know he's always outside the room waiting with a high five or else he says something, you know, that feels good to hear. I like that."

Call student after a bad day.

What usually happens when you've had a bad day with a student? Most teachers either avoid the student altogether or they keep reminding the student of the incident and continue rehashing it over and over again. Instead of these nonproductive responses, take advantage of another opportunity to build the relationship. Call the student at home and respond in a caring manner to the problem.

Here's what such a phone call might sound like:

Teacher: Paul, this is Mrs. Neilsen. I want to talk to you because I feel bad about the difficult day you and I had. I could see that it wasn't easy for you, either.

Student: *(Doesn't respond.)*

Teacher: Can you give me an idea of what was going on today? Why were you so upset?

Student: I don't know. Just a lousy day I guess.

Teacher: Is there anything I can do to help? Is there anything I'm doing that is a problem for you?

Student: Yeah, I've told you I can't do this math. I don't have enough time to finish and I can't understand it anyway. Why should I try to do all that work when I always get a bad grade anyhow? I'd rather talk to Pam and that's what I was doing.

Teacher: Paul, I want you to be successful in my class. I know you are capable of doing the work. You've shown me that before. The next time you feel that the work is too hard, let me know and I'll find a way to give you more help. How does that sound?

Student: Okay, I guess.

Teacher: Good. I don't think either of us wants to have more days like we had today. Tomorrow we're going to start over fresh. We'll work to make things better. How does that sound?

Student: Uh, yeah, all right.

Teacher: I'll see you tomorrow, then. And don't forget that if you're having any trouble you can come to me.

This phone call helps ensure that both of you begin the next day on a more positive note, and also demonstrates that you've taken an extra step to assure the student that you are there for him.

Here are some other techniques you can integrate throughout the year.

Relate to the student one-to-one.

Difficult students often need the one-to-one attention of a caring adult. Spend time talking with the student or involve yourself with the student in school activities. One way to relate to older students is to visit them on the job. Just showing up to say hello demonstrates your interest. Attending sports events in which they are participating is another way to reach out to these students.

Make home visits.

If appropriate, visit the student at home. It's a great opportunity to get an idea of the home environment and to relate to the student on his or her own turf.

We've talked about a variety of positive techniques you can use to send difficult students the message, "I care. I'm not going away."

Here's what else you need to do to communicate that message:

Hold Difficult Students Accountable

As much as difficult students need caring, they also need someone to hold them accountable. They need a balance between the trust you are building by reaching out to them and the limits you set and enforce.

> You can't establish two standards of behavior in your classroom—one for most of your students and one for the difficult ones.

You must stand your ground with difficult students and hold them accountable to the same rules and expectations as other students. Difficult students are accustomed to intimidating teachers into backing down on their limits. This is not in their best interest and does not demonstrate a commitment to their well being. By holding a student accountable you're teaching a life skill that this student must develop.

This story will illustrate what we mean.

> A teacher we know was dealing with an extremely hostile, very aggressive student who would not work. This student, Phil, wouldn't do any assignments. No homework. No class assignments. Nothing. Nothing the teacher said or any consequence she gave seemed to make any difference. Finally one day the teacher sat the student down and said very clearly and very firmly, "Phil, you're going to do your work today."
>
> As usual, Phil brushed her off: "I don't care what you say, I'm not going to do it." And at 3:00 when the dismissal bell rang, the student got up, walked out and got on the bus for home.
>
> Unbeknownst to Phil, however, the teacher had proactively worked out with his mom a plan of action to follow if he refused to work. He would miss the bus. He would not go home. He would finish his work. This teacher had done her planning. She had spoken with the parent and she had met with the administrator. She had the support of both.
>
> At 3:05 the teacher and the administrator went out and got Phil off the bus, brought him back to the class, and sat him down at his desk.
>
> "I told you that I expect you to do your assignments today. Now, get started."
>
> The student sat with a smirk on his face and said, "I don't care what you say. I told you, I'm not doing any work." Then Phil stretched back, put his feet out in the aisle and crossed his arms behind his head.

The teacher said nothing and went back to her desk to work on her lesson plans. She paid no further attention to Phil.

When 5:00 arrived Phil sat up with a big grin on his face. The teacher asked, "Phil, why are you smiling?"

He answered, "It's five o'clock. I know you're going home. I know you're going home and I haven't done my work. And there's nothin' you can do about it."

The teacher answered him calmly, "No one's won, Phil." She then took Phil with her to the office and called her husband (who had also been previously alerted). "I won't be home for awhile tonight. I've got to work late. Will you please bring me some dinner?"

Shortly thereafter her husband arrived with a hot meal. The teacher settled back at her desk, enjoying the meal. Phil just sat there.

Pretty soon it was 6:30. The teacher had finished eating and was once again engrossed in work at her desk.

By now Phil was tired and hungry. And what do you think he started doing? *He finally started to believe her.* He began to understand that this teacher meant business.

At 6:45 Phil opened a book and started working. By 8:00 he had finished. Phil had, indeed, completed his work that day.

After hearing this story, we decided to talk to Phil. we wanted to hear a student's perspective on this teacher's approach. His reply:

"She's not kidding around. She kept me here until 8:00. I couldn't believe it."

The teacher had sent Phil a very clear message:

> "Phil, I don't care how long it takes, you will do your work.
> If I have to stay here till 8:00 at night, I'll stay because
> you're going to succeed in my room. I don't like staying
> here any more than you do, but you're going to succeed in
> my room because I care about you succeeding."

This may be an extreme example, but this is what we are talking about with difficult students. They're used to teachers giving up and going away. They've got to understand and believe that you mean business. This teacher meant business and communicated it to her student. He got the message.

Chances are good that other students got the message, too. This is one teacher who means what she says. She cares about her students and she's committed to helping them succeed.

> Hold difficult students accountable. Let them know that you
> have just as high expectations for them as you do for other
> students. Do not make excuses for these students. Set firm,
> consistent limits and stick with them.

How successfully you deal with difficult students will be a direct result of your expectations. The point is this: You have choices. You can choose not to make home visits, not to call students before school begins, or not to greet students at the door. In the short term, this may be the easier road to follow. But what price will you pay? Life may be easier in the short run, but where will you be one month from now if you don't take these steps? Where will you be six months from now?

Difficult students *aren't* going away. You can be sure of that. Look at yourself down the road five years from now and decide if you want your situation to stay the same or if you want to make changes. Do you want to take control and guide your professional future to a more satisfying level?

> "Suddenly I saw myself five years from now. I was tired, burned out, and angry. My students didn't like me, I didn't like the way I was with them, and I was frustrated with my job. This wasn't the future I wanted, so I knew I had to make a choice. I could quit or I could make some changes. Teaching is my profession, though, and I still regard it as a unique opportunity to make a difference in this world. So I decided to take back my profession. I decided to make sure that the teacher I will be a year from now and five years from now is the teacher that makes me satisfied, happy and proud."

Expectations do create reality. If you look at your difficult students day in and day out and think, "I can't do anything about these kids," you're right. You won't be able to do anything. If the reality you see is one of doom and hopelessness, that will be your reality. And that is what you'll live every day.

If, however, you look at your students and see possibilities that excite and challenge you, that is the reality you will experience.

It's up to you.

SECTION ONE
Summary

Build trust.

Respond proactively.

Establish a positive relationship.

The success of every effort you make with a difficult student will ultimately depend upon the consistency and determination with which you pursue these objectives. All the technical skills in the world won't make a bit of difference if your difficult student has no trust in you and has developed no positive relationship with you.

These objectives are ongoing and will be interwoven throughout everything else presented in this book. Pay attention to them, act upon them, and you will be in a position to make major changes with the student.

You can succeed with difficult students.

MEETING THE SPECIAL NEEDS OF DIFFICULT STUDENTS

Meeting the Special Needs of Difficult Students

Reaching out to difficult students, and building positive relationships, require skilled use of specialized behavior management techniques. In Section Two of *Succeeding With Difficult Students* we will begin the process of individualizing your responses to difficult students' behavior.

Identifying the Primary Needs of Difficult Students

A sixth-grade teacher shared this observation about a student in her class:

> "Something's going on with Andrew that I don't see in my other students. It's more than just his behavior—his talking back and his refusal to do work. It's deeper than that. It's the frustration or neediness I feel behind these behaviors that disturbs me so much. It disturbs me because although I see that something's wrong, I don't know exactly what it is or what to do about it. The only thing I know for sure is that most approaches I try with Andrew backfire. If I give him positive attention he rejects it—in fact he behaves worse. If I hold him accountable with consequences, he doesn't blink an eye. I feel like this is a kid crying for help and I don't even know what he needs."

This teacher made a perceptive observation.

Difficult students bring more with them to school each day than the disruptive behaviors you see—the behaviors that interfere with your teaching and cause you so much stress.

Research shows that they also bring some very powerful psychological needs that they are driven to fulfill—basic needs that are not being adequately met in their lives.

- Some students are difficult because they need extra attention.
- Some students are difficult because they need firm limits.
- Some students are difficult because they need extra motivation.

It is the student's attempts to fulfill these needs in any manner possible that result in disruptive classroom behavior.

The sixth-grade teacher was correct. These students do need something extra from you that your other students don't need. They need a teacher to recognize that real unmet needs are prompting them to choose behaviors that are not in their best interest. And they need a teacher who will then give them what they need to appropriately fulfill these needs.

> Helping a student make better behavioral choices at school means first understanding what his or her motivation is to misbehave.

Until you accurately identify *why* a student misbehaves you cannot accurately identify what the student needs from you and what steps you can take to effectively meet the student's needs so that he or she will be less disruptive and more successful.

It wasn't until Andrew's teacher subsequently identified him as a student who needed firm limits that she was able to direct her behavior management efforts toward him in a manner to which he could respond.

Let's look now at the three needs that motivate a student to misbehave.

Some students are difficult because they need extra attention.

"Bradley's only one of thirty students in my class, but the minute he comes into the room he's the only one I seem to be able to see or hear. This child is always bothering me. He's constantly jumping out of his seat, tapping or touching other students, making irrelevant remarks or silly noises during class and interrupting me while I teach. He's not a bad kid; I don't think Bradley has a really mean bone in his body. But that doesn't change the fact that he's so disruptive I can barely get through a lesson. It's ironic; I've had students—really tough students—who didn't annoy me half as much as Bradley does. He just plain gets on my nerves with his continual distracting behavior."

Bradley needs attention.

Teachers today are seeing more and more students who, like Bradley, demand excessive attention. This may be a result of the increasing lack of human touch in society today—the increasing lack of one-on-one attention from caring adults in some students' lives. Whatever the cause, the result is the same. These kids need attention and will take any kind of attention they can get—even if they have to get in trouble to get it!

 ## Some students are difficult because they need firmer limits.

"With Jeff, the body language alone tells a story: *'Don't mess with me.'* This is one student who puts a lot of effort into intimidation. No matter what I ask him to do in class I get a belligerent challenge back: 'Man, I'm not gonna do this work so do yourself a favor and quit hassling me.' I've already sent him to the office several times but he doesn't care and nothing changes. The other day he put his feet up on the desk in front of him and just leaned back, staring at me—daring me to say something about it. And you know what? I didn't say anything. Nothing at all. It was easier not to. He knew it, I knew it, and 33 other students knew it."

Jeff needs firmer limits.

More than anything else, students like Jeff need adults who will care enough about them to let them know that their behavior is simply not acceptable. In the 90s, many kids are scared, rootless and without direction. The divorce rate is high, families are often fragmented, and students' lives often lack the structure that provides security and a sense of well being. Many of these students come from home environments where no limits are set—or where they have been abused in a manner that causes them to harbor a great deal of anger and resentment toward authority. Without limits, these students feel powerless; out of control. The environments in which they live demand toughness. Because they have no limits set for them, they have a need to control situations. These students need you to stop their downward spiral. These students need you to provide limits.

 ### Some students are difficult because they need motivation.

"Nicole's favorite phrase is 'I can't.' *I can't do this work. I can't make this diorama. I can't play soccer.* Well, I can't deal with this frustration much longer. If I try to get her to do her classwork, she cries. Then I have to spend the next fifteen minutes calming her down, making her feel better. When she doesn't bring in her homework, which is most of the time, she makes excuses about what happened to it. I know she can do the work I assign, but usually she won't even begin an assignment unless I practically pick up the pencil for her. Even then she doesn't complete anything. I guess I'm frustrated because I really don't know what to do with her."

Nicole needs motivation.

Where is this child's self-esteem? Confidence? Children with no self-esteem or confidence are adrift—sails without wind. They need an adult to build their self-esteem and confidence, to have high expectations and to provide them with encouragement. They need an adult to tell them, "Yes you can, I know you can, and I'll show you that you can!"

Many of these students would rather fail without making an effort than face the fear of failing with effort. These are students who don't take risks. Unless we intervene, we are dooming them to failure. After all, what does their behavior get them? They get out of taking responsibility for doing anything.

> The need for extra attention.
>
> The need for firmer limits.
>
> The need for extra motivation.

When a difficult student is disruptive or noncompliant, he or she is attempting to fulfill one of these needs.

And when teachers respond reactively or ineffectively to this disruptive behavior, they are often in fact fulfilling the student's need for attention, limits, or motivation, but in a way that does not help the student and instead further encourages inappropriate behavior.

In short, difficult students continue to engage in inappropriate behavior because they get something from it.

Let's take a look at scenes of Bradley, Jeff and Nicole in the classroom, and see the effects of their misbehavior—on them and on their teachers.

 Bradley: A Student Who Needs Attention

During a directed lesson, Bradley, an attention-seeking student, is sitting in the back of the room making silly noises.

Teacher: Okay, Bradley, that's enough! Quiet down, please.

Bradley complies and the teacher continues with her lesson. Within a few minutes, however, Bradley is at it again.

Teacher: Bradley, we all appreciate the sound effects; now please pay attention to what *I'm* saying.

The teacher tries to put the disruption to rest with humor. The class laughs along with Bradley, and the lesson continues. Soon, however, Bradley is out of his seat and poking another student.

Teacher: (*annoyed*) Bradley, get back into your seat. Now!

Bradley: But I dropped my pencil and it rolled under Christina's seat. I had to get it.

Teacher: Bradley, how many times do I have to keep reminding you to hang onto your things? You're wasting a lot of class time for all of us.

Bradley scrambles around, grabbing for his pencil on the floor. The class laughs. Bradley laughs. Then, back in his seat, Bradley intentionally drops his pencil once again. It doesn't roll, so he lightly kicks it and looks up to the teacher in a sheepish way.

Teacher: Okay, Bradley, that's it. Pick up your pencil and sit down. Class, let's continue . . .

Bradley needs attention from his peers and from his teacher. In this scenario, the teacher filled that need—she and the class gave Bradley what he needed most—attention. And what did he get that attention for? *Disruptive behavior.*

Why shouldn't Bradley act up in class? He's getting his need met. He's filling his attention quota.

Jeff: A Student Who Needs to Have Firmer Limits

A seventh-grade history teacher is getting his class started on a reading assignment.

Teacher: Class, I want you to open your books and begin reading Chapter 12. John and Sue, good job getting started. Lisa, that's the way. Jeff, please open your book, too.

Jeff: Forget it. I'm not opening my book to anything.

Teacher: Jeff, there's no need for that attitude. Just open your . . .

Jeff: Stuff it. If I wanted to read that cr... I'd have already read it.

Teacher: (*angrily*) There's no excuse whatsoever for using language like that in this classroom.

Jeff: Back off! Don't start messing with me today.

Teacher: (*shouting*) I'm warning you, Jeff, open your book and start reading, and that's that!

Jeff slams his book shut and shoves it off his desk and onto the floor.

Teacher: Fine. If you want to fail this class just sit there. Everyone else, please continue with your reading.

In this scenario, Jeff got what he needs most—control. He wants to be in charge.

Jeff is a student who needs firm, nonconfrontational limits, something he isn't getting at home or at school. Because of this, he constantly needs to test limits and confront the teacher's authority. By his angry, confrontational response, this teacher has gotten into a battle with Jeff that he can't really win. Consequently, this teacher has given Jeff control. Jeff has had his need fulfilled.

Nicole: A Student Who Needs Extra Motivation

A first-grade teacher is starting the class on an art project.

Teacher: Nicole, are you ready to begin?

Nicole: I can't do this.

Teacher: Sure you can, Nicole. Just get out your scissors and start cutting.

Nicole: No, I can't. I've never made one of these before. I know I can't do it right.

Teacher: Nicole, won't you please just try? You'll do fine.

The teacher goes away for a few moments. When she returns, Nicole has done nothing.

Teacher: Come on, Nicole, you can do this. It's easy.

Nicole: No I can't. I tried. And it didn't work.

Nicole starts crying. The teacher picks up the scissors and paper and begins to cut.

Teacher: Look Nicole, I'll show you. See, all you do is cut along the outline. Here, it's already half done.

Nicole: (*crying*) I can't. I told you it's too hard.

Teacher: Okay, Nicole. Take a minute to stop crying. You can try it again later.

Nicole has no self-confidence. By her sympathetic but ineffective response, the teacher is demonstrating that she doesn't have high expectations for Nicole, either. By patronizing and placating Nicole, the teacher is actually enabling her failure. What does Nicole get out of all this? She doesn't do the work.

What happened in these scenes?

Bradley got attention, which is what he wanted.

Jeff got control, which he wanted.

And Nicole didn't have to do anything . . . which suits her just fine.

In each case the teacher fell back on reactive responses that played into the student's agenda. These students' needs were filled, but in a manner that was not beneficial to them and which will only serve to motivate them to continue the disruptive behavior.

What can you do?

You can't change a student's primary need, but you can redirect it. You can learn to work with a disruptive student in a manner that both meets his or her need *and* encourages better behavior.

Identify a difficult student's primary need.

With that information, you can then proceed to individualize your behavior management efforts in a manner that *this particular student* will respond to.

How do you identify a student's primary need?

You do it by looking at:

1) the student's behavior,

2) your response to that behavior, and

3) the student's response to your response.

Here's what we mean:

Identifying a Student Who Needs Extra Attention

Look at the student's behavior:

This student continually engages in behavior that demands excessive attention from you and/or other students. Behaviors associated with the attention-seeking student include non-malicious actions such as making silly noises in class, getting out of seat, irrelevant comments, horsing around, poking or touching other students, making faces, shouting out, and any other non-threatening, attention-getting devices kids can use.

Look at your response to the student's behavior:

Students who need attention *annoy* you. They get on your nerves and drive you crazy with their incessant "Hey, look at me" behavior.

Finally, look at the student's reaction to your response:

The student will stop disrupting when given attention, but will very soon start engaging in disruptive behavior, demanding more attention.

If you have a student who fits this profile,
he or she is a student who needs extra attention.

Identifying a Student Who Needs Firm Limits

Look at the student's behavior:

A student who needs firmer limits constantly challenges you or other students, talks back to you in front of other students, argues with you, lies, or verbally or physically fights with other students. These students may simply refuse to do what they are told. They are in a power struggle with you. They want to be in control.

Look at your response to the student's behavior:

Students who are constantly testing limits make you angry. Their continual belligerent, hostile responses make it easy to get into an escalating, confrontational argument.

Finally, look at the student's reaction to your response:

In response to anger, this student will cause a confrontation, refuse to comply and argue.

If you have a student who fits this profile,
he or she is a student who needs firm limits.

Identifying a Student Who Needs Motivation

Look at the student's behavior:

Behaviors associated with the need for extra motivation include refusal to begin assignments, failure to complete assignments, giving up easily, an "I can't" attitude, and continually making excuses.

Look at your response to the student's behavior:

Frustration. With these students you try everything you know, but nothing seems to work.

Finally, look at the student's reaction to your response:

The student still does not do the work. Nothing works.

If you have a student who fits this profile,
he or she is a student who needs extra motivation.

Until you identify the underlying need that is prompting a difficult student's disruptive behavior, you cannot go further in creating an individualized plan for helping that student—*and* you leave yourself open to reactive, detrimental responses to that behavior.

> Remember, reacting to a student's primary need is only going to prolong or escalate the disruptive behavior.

And after you've identified the primary need?

Set goals for appropriately fulfilling the student's primary need.

Once you have identified a difficult student's primary need, you can begin to set goals that will address this need in a positive and more beneficial manner.

Here then are specific goals for each of the three primary needs.

Goal for Students Who Need Attention:

Give massive amounts of positive attention for appropriate behavior.

Remember, these students want attention—good or bad, planned or unplanned. They will take what they can get. In order to help this type of student succeed, it's up to you to plan to give the student the maximum amount of *positive* attention in the shortest amount of time, so the need for negative consequences (attention) comes only as a last resort.

Let's look at a scenario with Bradley once more. This time, however, the teacher will approach Bradley in a proactive manner that recognizes his needs as an attention-seeking student.

Scene: The teacher is about to begin a directed lesson. She knows she can expect disruptive behavior from Bradley, so she has planned to both remind him of the appropriate behavior she expects and to give him the attention he needs for positive behavior rather than negative.

Before beginning the lesson, the teacher walks over to Bradley's desk. She speaks to him quietly and in a friendly manner.

Teacher: Bradley, remember the directions for listening to a lesson: Eyes on me, pencil and notebook out, no talking. If you have a question, raise your hand. Okay? (*she smiles*) Good.

Having reminded Bradley of the directions, and having given him some attention, the teacher begins her lesson. Almost immediately she gives Bradley more positive attention for being on task.

Teacher: Bradley's ready to listen.

As she proceeds with the lesson, the teacher circulates the classroom. This gives her an opportunity from time to time to stand near Bradley and give him a nod, a smile or a pat on the back for staying on task. More attention for positive behavior.

Later, as Bradley begins to fidget, she gets his attention (and gives him attention) by mentioning his name within the lesson.

Teacher: Okay, let's say that Bradley and Debra were outfitting a Conestoga wagon for the journey on the Oregon Trail . . .

Throughout the lesson, the teacher continues to make a point of recognizing Bradley for appropriate behavior. She makes sure that Bradley receives attention for his appropriate behavior before he even has time to be disruptive.

Understanding that Bradley needs this extra attention enables the teacher to proactively plan how she will respond to his behavior.

And Bradley is learning that he can receive even more satisfying attention for appropriate behavior.

Goal for Students Who Need Limits:

Provide very firm and consistent limits.

These students need to be provided very, very firm and consistent limits in a non-confrontational way. Non-confrontational because confrontation feeds their need to be big, tough and defiant. You must always work with these students in a way that allows them to save face in the classroom— even when you're setting limits.

Now let's replay a scene with Jeff. This time the teacher will approach Jeff in a manner that recognizes him as a student who needs firm limits.

> Scene: A seventh-grade history teacher is getting his class started on a reading assignment. Before the lesson, he quietly reminds Jeff, a disruptive student, of the directions for the activity. He does so in an unobtrusive way that does not attract the attention of other students.

> Teacher: *(quietly)* Jeff, remember that the directions for independent reading are no talking, book on desk.

> Jeff: I don't feel like reading today.

> Teacher: I understand, Jeff, but I want you to take your book out and start reading.

> Jeff: Aw get off it. Just leave me alone!

> Teacher: *(very calmly)* I hear you're upset. I hear that you don't want to do your work. But doing your assignment is your job in this class and you need to get started.

> Jeff: I said I don't want to.

> Teacher: *(speaking very quietly)* Jeff, there's no talking back in this classroom. That's a warning. You have a choice now. Either get started on your assignment or you'll choose to stay one minute after class today.

> Jeff mumbles under his breath, but takes out the book.

> As the students begin reading, the teacher stays close by Jeff.

> After a few minutes of reading, Jeff happens to look up and the teacher quietly nods. In a completely

nonconfrontational manner he stays with him. He doesn't retreat. He's as strong as Jeff is defiant. And because all of his signals to Jeff are understated and unobtrusive, the teacher gives him no need to act up to save face. Jeff stays on task.

After class, the teacher quietly speaks to Jeff as he's leaving the room.

Teacher: Good job.

Note: Students who need limits are often very tough students. If Jeff had responded more defiantly the teacher would, of course, had to have taken additional steps in dealing with him. We will be addressing these issues in upcoming chapters.

 Goal for Students Who Need Motivation:

Focus all behavioral management efforts toward getting the student to do work.

Before class, during class and after class, let these students know you have confidence in their ability to do their work. Always maintain high expectations for these students and let them know that you have high expectations. If need be, break assignments down to manageable parts and strive to get that student starting and completing the assignments with the rest of the class. Offer this student the maximum amount of motivation you possibly can to encourage him or her to do any kind of work possible. All corrective actions towards this student must be focused toward getting him or her to do the work. If the work isn't getting done in class, it must be done at another time.

Let's replay a scene with Nicole. This time we will see her teacher enable her to succeed with the lesson, not enable her to get out of doing the work.

Scene: A teacher is introducing a cut-and-paste activity to her first graders. She knows Nicole needs extra motivation, so she's planned to give her the encouragement and structure she needs.

Teacher: Nicole, are you ready to begin? Do you have your scissors?

Nicole: I can't do this. I can't cut anything out right.

Teacher: Sure you can, Nicole. Here, let's try this. I'm going to mark an X here on the pattern and an X here. Now I know you can cut between these two X's.

The teacher breaks the task down into small parts.

Nicole: No, I can't. I know I can't do it right.

Teacher: Nicole, you have a choice. You can do your work now, or you can finish it during lunchtime, after you've eaten. The choice is yours.

Given this choice, Nicole cuts from X to X.

Teacher: Nicole, that's perfect! Look at what a great job you did. Right on the line! You're going to make a beautiful pattern. Now let's make another X and cut even farther, okay?

The teacher gives plenty of praise for any attempted effort toward completion of the job.

Important: Another reason for misbehavior is that work given to the student is not at the appropriate level for the student, or the student has a learning disability that prevents him or her from being able to do the work. If the student is truly not capable of doing the academic work, nothing in this book is going to be effective in motivating him or her to try to do the work.

CHAPTER 6

Teaching Appropriate Behavior

"I know Cindy needs attention. And I know I have to give her the attention she needs for her *appropriate* behavior. The trouble is, I just don't see that much appropriate behavior to reinforce. All day long she does one thing after another to make me or the other students stop and pay attention to her. No matter what we're doing, she has to be center stage, and it's disruptive to everyone."

Once you've identified the primary need of a difficult student, it's time to individualize further and proactively plan very concrete steps to help that student improve his or her behavior.

First, you need to *teach* your student the appropriate behavior that you expect.

Why teach behavior?

With difficult students, it probably seems as though you spend all day long, day after day, repeating the same directions over and over again.

"Cindy, take your book to your reading group and sit down!"

It's frustrating. All of your other students seem to be able to remember how to work independently, how to transition, how to line up for recess, or how to take a test, but for some reason your difficult students just don't do what you expect them to do.

The fact is this: Many difficult students just don't know how to behave, or may not understand your expectations for different activities. If they are ever going to be successful in your class they need to be taught (or retaught) appropriate behavior for the specific activities in which they misbehave.

But what if they seem to misbehave <u>all</u> of the time?

> "Cindy is always off task. All day long I have to tell her to get to work or stop talking. It never lets up."

> "When Bobby comes to class, he's a non-stop interruption. He's constantly clowning around and making a spectacle of himself. He never sits still!"

> "Jerome is totally unmanageable, I don't know how he gets dressed in the morning. There's never a time I tell him to do something that he doesn't talk back and argue with me about it. The boy's a constant battle."

Are difficult students really off task all of the time?

It may feel that way to you, but in fact difficult students are not constantly disruptive. Even the *most* disruptive of students do not disrupt more than 25% of the time.

- Cindy really does stop talking some of the time.

- Bobby in fact does sit still some of the time.

- And Jerome doesn't talk back every single time you speak to him.

To help your difficult student be more successful, focus on that "25%-or-less" time. Identify the exact circumstances in which he or she behaves inappropriately.

Start developing a behavior profile on the student.

The best way to define which behaviors to focus on is to establish a behavior profile on the student. This profile includes the following information:

1) The activities during which the student is noncompliant

2) The specific problem behaviors that occur during those activities

3) The *appropriate* behaviors you want the student to engage in

Steps to Follow When Developing a Behavior Profile on a Student

As we go through each of the steps, you will see examples of behavior profiles on three students, Cindy, a second grader, Bobby, a fifth grader, and Jerome, a tenth grader.

Step 1: Determine when problems occur.

To teach a student appropriate behavior, you first need to find out during which activities the student is actually behaving inappropriately. Based on the student's primary need, you will find that certain classroom activities throughout the day provide maximum opportunities for inappropriate, noncompliant behavior.

A student who needs attention is likely to be noncompliant when he or she can't get your attention. For example:

- when you're with a group and the student is supposed to be working independently.

- when you are working one-on-one with another student.

 A student who needs firm limits is likely to be noncompliant when you ask him to do something or function in an unstructured situation. For example:

- during transitions.

- when working in cooperative learning groups.

- when asked to follow any direction.

 A student who needs motivation is likely to be noncompliant when asked to do academic work.

By observing a difficult student for a day or two you will be able to note exactly when off-task behaviors normally take place.

In the following examples, notice that in each of the behavior profiles the teacher has pinpointed several activities during which noncompliant behaviors occur.

Behavior Profile: Cindy—Grade 2

When Student Is Noncompliant	What Behaviors Take Place	Behaviors Needed
Entering the classroom		
Lining up after recess		
Moving into small groups		

Behavior Profile: Bobby—Grade 5

When Student Is Noncompliant	What Behaviors Take Place	Behaviors Needed
Independent seatwork		
Class discussion		
Learning groups		

Behavior Profile: Jerome—Grade 10

When Student Is Noncompliant	What Behaviors Take Place	Behaviors Needed
Independent seatwork Lecture		

Step 2: Define the problem behaviors.

What exactly is going on when the student is noncompliant? Is he talking out? Is she continually getting out of her seat? Is he shoving other students?

Be specific. List only *observable* inappropriate behaviors. Vaguely stated problems will only result in vague solutions. Be accurate. What are the behaviors you really observe?

Vague observations:	Specific observable behaviors:
Doesn't act nice	Hits classmates
Has a bad attitude	Shouts out
Messes around too much	Does not remain seated
Acts silly	Curses

By being specific in your assessments, your image of what exactly is going on with each student gets sharper and begins to take form.

Behavior Profile: Cindy—Grade 2

When Student Is Noncompliant	What Behaviors Take Place	Behaviors Needed
Entering the classroom	Runs into room, talks to friends, does not take seat.	
Lining up after recess	Continues to play after the bell rings, pushing and shoving while in line.	
Moving into small groups	Does not go straight to group, stops to talk with friends, forgets materials.	

Behavior Profile: Bobby—Grade 5

When Student Is Noncompliant	What Behaviors Take Place	Behaviors Needed
Independent seatwork	Argues when asked to work, talks, gets out of seat.	
Class discussion	Speaks without raising hand, disruptive remarks, out of seat.	
Learning groups	Out of seat, pokes other students, draws pictures, disruptive conversation.	

Behavior Profile: Jerome—Grade 10

When Student Is Noncompliant	What Behaviors Take Place	Behaviors Needed
Independent seatwork	Talks, bothers other students.	
Lecture	Distracts other students (passing notes, touching, laughing, disparaging remarks).	

Step 3: Now plan what you want the student to do.

Students can't be expected to meet your behavioral expectations if they don't know what those expectations are. Now that you have defined the student's *inappropriate* behavior during a specific activity, what specific *appropriate* behaviors are needed for the student to be successful?

> Plan exactly how you expect the student to behave during the activity.

Behavior Profile: Cindy—Grade 2

When Student Is Noncompliant	What Behaviors Take Place	Behaviors Needed
Entering the classroom	Runs into room, talks to friends, does not take seat.	Walk into room, go straight to seat, no talking.
Lining up after recess	Continues to play after the bell rings, pushing and shoving while in line.	Freeze when bell rings, walk immediately to classroom, line up single file outside door, keep hands to self, no talking.
Moving into small groups	Does not go straight to group, stops to talk with friends, forgets materials.	When given direction to go to small groups, gather all materials, walk straight to group, sit down, no talking.

Behavior Profile: Bobby—Grade 5

When Student Is Noncompliant	What Behaviors Take Place	Behaviors Needed
Independent seatwork	Argues when asked to work, talks, gets out of seat.	Begin assignment when given direction, eyes on work, no talking, raise hand if need help.
Class discussion	Speaks without raising hand, disruptive remarks, out of seat.	Raise hand to ask a question, stay in seat, speak only when called upon.
Learning groups	Out of seat, pokes other students, draws pictures, disruptive conversation.	Stay in seat, keep hands to self, work only on assignment, talk only about the assignment.

Behavior Profile: Jerome—Grade 10

When Student Is Noncompliant	What Behaviors Take Place	Behaviors Needed
Independent seatwork	Talks, bothers other students.	Eyes on paper, no talking, raise hand to ask a question.
Lecture	Distracts other students (passing notes, touching, laughing, disparaging remarks).	Eyes on teacher, no talking, raise hand to speak or ask a question, keep hands to self.

The behavior profile is complete when you've identified when noncompliant behavior occurs, what the problem behaviors are, and what behaviors you expect of your student.

Now you're ready to teach the student the needed behaviors.

- Cindy needs to be taught how to enter the classroom, line up for recess, and move into small groups.

- Bobby needs to be taught how to behave during independent seatwork, class discussions, and when he is in a learning group.

- Jerome needs to be taught how to behave during independent seatwork and during a lecture.

> As you develop a behavior profile on a difficult student, you will usually find inappropriate behavior showing up in more than one activity or situation.

Do not attempt to teach behavior for all activities at one time.

Start slowly. Pick the one that is most disruptive or bothersome to you, the one that really drives you crazy, and focus on it first. Later, as the student's behavior improves in one area, you can teach appropriate behavior for another.

But what about the really tough students? What's this going to do for them?

> "My students are so tough, I don't see how teaching them how to sit down, teaching them how to follow directions, or teaching them how to walk into a room is going to solve any problems. You've got to be kidding! You haven't met my students!"

With really tough students, teaching behavior may not *solve* the problem, but it's the first step you must take. It's going to take a number of steps to be successful with these students, and we'll be adding on these steps in upcoming chapters. But to succeed at all, it's up to you to first give the student the "basic training" he or she needs from which to build success.

After all, if a student doesn't know how to behave during an activity, what are his or her chances of ever succeeding in that activity? You may have to take further steps with a student—but the process still must begin with teaching appropriate behavior.

Teach the appropriate behavior.

When you take the time to teach a difficult student appropriate behavior you are not only proactively preventing problems from continuing, but you are also showing the student that you care enough to do what needs to be done to help him or her succeed.

It's a vote of confidence that a difficult student needs. It says, "I believe that you can do it, and I'm going to help you."

It helps the student take another step back up toward the Trust Line.

The following scenarios will demonstrate how to teach appropriate behavior to students grades K-3, grades 4-6 and grades 7-12.

> Keep this in mind: The younger the age of the difficult student,
> the more crucial it is to actually teach and re-teach him or her
> the appropriate behaviors needed to be successful.

Teaching Appropriate Behavior—Grades K-3

Expected behavior for entering the classroom

Step 1: Meet with the student one-on-one, when no other students are around. Speak calmly and with caring.

"Cindy, lately I've noticed that you've been having trouble coming into the classroom when the bell rings. You've been running into the room, visiting with friends, and you know what happens? When we're ready to get started with class you're not in your seat. I know you can do a better job than that."

Step 2: Model the behavior you want the student to engage in.

"I'm going to help you learn to come into the classroom correctly. First, I want you to watch me. I'm going to come into the classroom correctly and take my seat, just as if I were a student in this class. Will you watch me carefully?"

Teacher models the correct behavior. She then returns to Cindy.

"Okay, Cindy, did you see what I did? I walked into the room. I went straight to my seat and I sat down. Then I took my book out and waited quietly. Do you think you could do that?"

Step 3: Have the student practice that behavior.

"Now why don't you practice coming into the classroom just like I did?"

Student practices the correct behavior.

Step 4: Reinforce the student for engaging in the appropriate behavior.

"That's excellent, Cindy. That's exactly how you need to come into the room. I'll be watching tomorrow morning to see if you remember everything we've practiced—I know you'll do a good job of following these directions."

Throughout the next day, and the days following, this teacher makes a point of positively reinforcing Cindy when she enters the classroom appropriately.

Teaching Appropriate Behavior—Grades 4-6

Expected behavior during independent work time

Step 1: **Meet with the student one-on-one, when no other students are around. Speak calmly and with caring.**

"Bobby, I'd like to talk with you for a few minutes about your work habits during independent work time."

Step 2: **Explain the rationale for why the student should engage in the behavior.**

"It's important that you work quietly during independent work time. When you talk to other students you not only keep them from doing their work, but you also don't get your own work done. That doesn't help you in school, does it? You've had trouble finishing your assignments lately, and this is part of the reason why. I want to help you make a change for the better."

Step 3: **Tell the student the exact behavior you want him or her to engage in.**

"Okay, Bobby, let's review the directions I expect you to follow during independent work time. During independent work time I expect you to remain in your seat, no talking, and have only the materials you need on your desk. If you have a question, raise your hand and I will come and help you. Do you have any questions about that?"

Step 4: **Have the student repeat or write down the behaviors he or she is to engage in.**

"Can you repeat to me what I expect you to do during independent work time?"

Student repeats the directions.

"Good. Now tomorrow when I assign your independent work I expect to see you follow those directions. I'm sure you can do it with no problem."

Teaching Appropriate Behavior—Grades 7-12

Expected behavior during a lecture

Step 1: Meet with the student one-on-one, when no other students are around.

"Jerome, can you please wait after class for a moment? I'd like to talk with you."

Step 2: In a very matter-of-fact manner, specify the exact behaviors you expect.

"Jerome, you didn't make very good choices today about how to behave when I was giving a lecture to the class. I want to take a moment to review the directions we have for listening to a lecture: Eyes on me, no talking. If you have a question or want to speak, raise your hand and I will call on you.

"Do you have any questions about those directions? Good. I know I'll see improvement when we have another lecture on Wednesday. See you tomorrow."

Though the approach varies slightly for different grade levels, the results are the same. By proactively teaching the appropriate behaviors you expect, your chances for helping these students succeed are greatly increased.

Remind students of appropriate behavior before the activity takes place.

Teaching appropriate behavior is a first step, but proactive teachers don't leave it at that. They know that a difficult student will need constant reminding and reinforcement if he or she is going to successfully and consistently replace inappropriate behavior with appropriate behavior.

> The more clearly you spell out your expectations, the more likely the student will be to meet them.

Therefore, proactive teachers use the behavior profile to cue themselves to when a student is most likely to engage in noncompliant behavior— and then they step in to give the student a helping hand.

Plan Book Reminder

Writing a reminder to yourself in your plan book is a great way to make sure you stay on top of the situation. For example, if you have taught Bobby the appropriate behavior you expect during a class discussion, whenever you are planning a discussion just jot a note to yourself in your plan book to remind Bobby of the behavior you expect.

Subject	*Social Studies*	
MONDAY	Chapter 6 Discuss questions on pgs. 112-114 Remind Bobby of approp. behavior	

Later in the week, when the activity takes place, you'll have a reminder waiting for you.

For example:

Cindy's profile shows that she has a difficult time when she is in a small group situation. Knowing this, and having taught Cindy the expected behaviors, her teacher goes over to Cindy before any small-group activity and quietly reminds her of the behaviors she needs to choose. This little reminder gives Cindy the nudge she often needs to stay on task.

> Teacher: (*calmly, gently*) Cindy, remember, when I give the direction to go to your group, I expect you to take your book, paper and pencil, walk straight to your group, sit down and no talking.

Bobby's profile shows that he is particularly prone to disruptive behavior when everyone is working independently. Whenever students are given an independent assignment, his teacher takes a moment to very quietly, and in a low-key manner, go over to him and reiterate the directions.

> Teacher: (*calmly, quietly*) Bobby, remember that during independent work time I expect you to remain in your seat, work on your assignment and not talk. If you have a question, raise your hand and I'll come help you. Okay?

Jerome's profile shows that he is often disruptive when the class is taking a test. His teacher has taught him the behavior he needs to choose, but she still takes the opportunity to very quietly remind him of that behavior before a test. She doesn't call attention to Jerome, but nevertheless she gets her message across.

> Teacher: (*very quietly and low-keyed*) Jerome, during the test today I expect you to keep your eyes on your paper and no talking. If you have a question raise your hand.

By planning ahead, by knowing when disruptions may occur, you can defuse potential problems by reminding students of your expectations. You also are giving the student another opportunity to succeed.

Remember: Your goal is to prevent problems before they begin. That's what proactive responses are all about.

7

Providing Positive Support

"Gary has been in trouble ever since he came to this school as a second-grader. He's been passed along year after year by teachers who haven't really wanted him in their classes. Well, he's in my class this year, and I'm not going to be one more teacher who lets him down. If I'm going to turn things around for him I have to do something to balance the negative attention he's used to receiving with a lot of positive attention when he behaves appropriately.

"If I don't give him attention when he's good, I'll sure be giving it to him when he's not. Gary's going to take my time one way or the other. I'd rather spend that time productively.

"My number-one goal for Gary this year is to build his self-esteem and trust by letting him know that I genuinely appreciate any effort he puts into better behavior in class. And I can't wait until I see perfect behavior before I give him this positive recognition. I'm going to have to take baby steps with Gary, and focus on improvement, not results. Every instinct this kid has tells him not to trust me. I have to let him know, every day, that I'm there beside him every step of the way. If I don't, nothing else I do will matter anyway.

"This year he'll have someone on his side."

You've taught the appropriate behavior you want from a difficult student. Now, what can you do to motivate him or her to choose that behavior?

When you're dealing with difficult students, you're dealing with students who have low self-esteem. The majority of the attention these students have received from adults, both at home and at school, has probably been negative. They may have been put down, beaten down, verbally or physically abused, laughed at for their efforts or criticized for their lack of efforts.

> Because of their negative experiences, and the lack of trust and low self-esteem these experiences produce, it is absolutely critical that difficult students are given massive positive support when they choose appropriate behavior.

Consistent and meaningful encouragement and reinforcement is important for all students, but it is crucial for difficult students.

To keep building a positive relationship, you need to take every opportunity that comes your way to demonstrate your confidence and high expectations.

> If you're ever going to really change a student's behavior, it is your positive interactions that will have the most powerful and lasting impact.

There will be times, of course, when corrective actions will be needed to stop a difficult student's unwanted behavior, and that will be addressed in Chapter 9. But keep in mind that only positive support has the power to *change* behavior. And that is the result you are after.

As you consider positives for your own students, keep this in mind: The more serious a student's problems have been, the more frequently that student needs to receive praise and positive recognition from you.

Support the behavior you want repeated.

Once you've taught a difficult student the appropriate behaviors you expect, you need to immediately turn to positive reinforcement to motivate the student to choose these behaviors.

Positive interactions are so important they cannot be left to chance. They must be planned and used systematically. But before we talk about when and how to use positive reinforcement with your difficult students, first let's address a roadblock that might stand in the way of increasing your positive interactions with them.

If positive support is so good for students, why are the majority of a teacher's responses to difficult students negative?

Positive reinforcement is not a new concept to educators. Teachers are well aware that it is a vital part of any classroom behavior management plan. But even though we know we need to be more positive with students, we tend instead to be negative with them. This is especially true with difficult students.

It's not that we *intend* to be negative—we *tend* to be negative!

This tendency is caused by our own physiology.

Look at the "anxiety" scale below. On a scale of 0 to 100, at 0 there's no anxiety at all. In fact, you're about to go to sleep. At the other end of the scale, at 100, you're having a panic attack. Your heart is racing wildly and you're struggling to keep control.

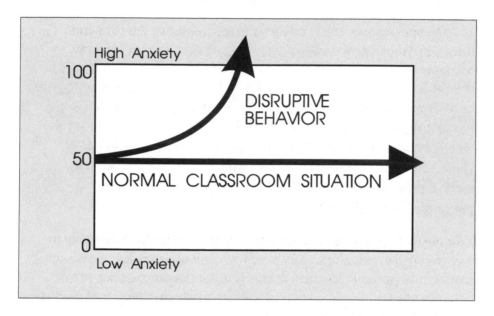

High Anxiety

100

DISRUPTIVE
BEHAVIOR

50

NORMAL CLASSROOM SITUATION

0

Low Anxiety

Now, when you are teaching your class and things are going all right, you're probably somewhere around 50 on the anxiety scale. What happens, though, when one of your students disrupts? When he or she is defiant, talks back or confronts you?

Your anxiety rises—sharply and quickly.

Why do you respond this way? Why does the disruptive behavior of even just one student cause such a rise in anxiety?

What's the greatest fear teachers have in the classroom? *Losing control.* With younger students, losing control might mean the thought of 35 children laughing, screaming, jumping out of their seats and running around the room. With older students, losing control carries with it very real implications of confrontational, defiant, even physically dangerous behavior.

While you may not actually *expect* to lose control, just the subconscious thought of a roomful of noncompliant, defiant students can send anxiety soaring when disruptions occur. Disruptive behavior, even of one student, causes a very real physiological response: anxiety.

What happens next? Your body's natural responses take over and your brain tells you to do something, anything at all to stop the anxiety you feel.

As a result, you react. You might shout at your student to behave or you might provide a disciplinary consequence—anything to lower your anxiety level. You might get angry, frustrated, or confontational.

> "John, stop fooling around right now. I've had it with you. I'm going to see you after class."

It's a physiological response, therefore, that leads teachers not only to leap reactively on disruptive behavior when it appears, but, more importantly perhaps, to be on the lookout for it. Because disruptive behavior produces such anxiety, a teacher is driven to stop it from ever occuring by keeping an eye out for it.

> Thus, we are physiologically driven to walk around the classroom looking for kids who are doing things we don't want them to do.

We look for *negative* behavior.

On the other hand, what happens when the class is well-behaved and everything is going smoothly? Your anxiety level drops, but at a very slow rate—so slowly you may not even notice it. Your body issues no sense of urgency prompting you to take action of any kind. Your body doesn't tell you to "quick, find appropriate behavior and recognize it!"

Think about this for a moment:

> Picture yourself circulating your own classroom, watching your students as they work. Who are you really looking for? The student over in the corner who is quietly doing his or her assignment? Or students who are off task and threaten to become disruptive?

We are thus prompted by our own bodies to pay attention to negative behavior and overlook positive behavior. We are physiologically driven to look for students who are doing things we don't want them to do.

This physiological reaction often stands in the way of being more positive with students. If you are going to take the positive steps you need to take with difficult students, you have to get past this roadblock.

What can you do to combat this tendency to look for the negative?

Be aware that physiologically you are driven to focus on the innapropriate, disruptive behavior of difficult students. If you don't make this shift in perception, you will not be able to change how you deal with these students. With that awareness you then need to develop skills that will prompt or cue you to look for the positive behavior of your difficult students.

This cannot be a vague, well-intentioned effort. You need to have a concrete plan for how you will provide more consistent praise to your difficult students.

Planning Is the Key

Teachers who provide massive and consistent positive attention to difficult students, at the right times and in a manner that best meets the students' needs, do not do so by chance. They set goals, and then plan how to meet these goals.

Let's start the planning process by first looking at the difficult student's behavior profile below—and seeing how it can help a teacher plan to be positive with a difficult student.

Behavior Profile: Kirk

When Student Is Noncompliant	What Behaviors Take Place	Behaviors Needed
Learning groups	In and out of seat, talking, poking and touching other students.	Stay in seat, keep hands to self, work only on assignment, talk only about the assignment.
Independent seatwork	Talks, in and out of seat, argues when asked to work.	Begin assignment when given direction, eyes on work, no talking, raise hand if needs help.

This profile tells us these things about Kirk:

- The activities during which Kirk's noncompliant behaviors occur

- The specific inappropriate behaviors Kirk engages in

- The specific appropriate behaviors Kirk needs to be taught and reinforced for

Kirk's teacher, by reviewing this behavior profile, knows at a glance just when he needs to beef up his use of positives with this student. (Remember, support the behavior you want repeated!)

In this case, the teacher knows that Kirk typically disrupts when the class is divided into learning groups and is working independently. He has therefore taught Kirk the appropriate behaviors he expects. And because he wants to help Kirk change his behavior, he must plan to intervene with positives to encourage Kirk to choose that behavior *before* Kirk has the opportunity to disrupt.

The teacher must be on the lookout for positive behavior.

- Provide massive amounts of positive support.

- Provide that positive support during those times when you want to reinforce improved, appropriate behavior.

Once you know when to target your positive support, set goals for yourself to deliver that support.

Set Goals for Positively Recognizing a Student's Appropriate Behavior

A day in class, or a period, goes by quickly and it's all too easy to intend to give positive support and then not get around to it. Here's one way to make sure that a difficult student gets the daily positive recognition he or she needs.

Set a goal that, for example, Amanda is going to receive 10 positive recognitions from you each day. As the day proceeds, you know that you've got to look for and find 10 examples of appropriate behavior from her. (With older students the goal may be 3 or 4 recognitions during a period.)

Having a goal will prompt you to actively look for good behavior rather than overlook it. And your behavior profile on the student will cue you as to when you should target giving the positives.

Here are some tips that will help you meet your goals:

1. Use your plan book.

When you plan for your lessons, also plan for the postive support you are going to give a difficult student. In your lesson plan book, write notes that will cue you to meet your goals during specific times of the day or during specific activities.

For example:

Subject:	Social Studies	
MONDAY	All groups cooperatively solve problem on p. 98. HW: quest. 8-16 p. 101 * Kirk/praise approp. behavior in groups (10 positives today!)	

Throughout the day keep track of meeting your positives goal by putting pen or pencil dots by the student's name.

2. Place reminders in your classroom.

Put a sign near the clock in the classroom reminding yourself that the time is always right to look for good behavior. Every time you glance at the clock you'll receive a friendly nudge to give positive support.

3. Watch it!

If you wear a wristwatch, place a small "sticker" dot on the watch face. Throughout the day, whenever you look at your watch you'll get a signal to give a positive.

4. Ten Coins in the Pocket

Here's a "cents"ible and unique way to remind yourself of your goals to positively recognize a difficult student—and to keep track of it. Here's how it works:

> Miss Johnson set a goal for herself to recognize Eric's appropriate behavior ten times during the day. To keep herself on track she put ten pennies in one of her pockets. The jingling of the coins served as a reminder throughout the day. Each time she gave Eric positive reinforcement, she moved one coin to the other pocket. When all the coins had been transferred she knew she had met her goal.

5. Walk around and look for positive behavior.

Don't just stay seated at your desk—stay in motion. Move around the classroom looking for good behavior. When you spot good behavior, comment on it.

Selecting and Implementing Positive Reinforcement

What is meaningful positive reinforcement to one student may not be as significant to another. It is important, therefore, to individualize your use of positives as much as possible. You will find that some students respond best to praise while others need the immediate gratification of a material reward. As you continue to build a positive relationship with a difficult student you will be better able to determine what will be most motivating to him or her.

Positive reinforcers discussed on the following pages include:

- Praise
- Positive notes and phone calls home
- Special privileges
- Behavior awards
- Tangible rewards

Praise

Praise is the easiest form of positive reinforcement to give and, for many students, the most effective. Personal words of support, enthusiasm and caring are exactly what many difficult students need to hear.

Praise Students According To Their Different Needs

Nick is an extremely confrontational student who needs firm limits. His teacher has been working to help him behave more appropriately during class discussions. Nick knows the behaviors his teacher expects—his teacher has taught them—and now she's making a point to reinforce him when he's engaging in those appropriate behaviors.

As a class discussion takes place, she's very aware when he's on task and making good choices. Because she understands the importance of positive support, she naturally wants to recognize him for his efforts. So in front of the rest of the students she proudly says, "Great job, Nick. You're following the directions perfectly." She smiles at him, but Nick glares back at her. Her praise rejected, the teacher feels hurt and confused. Suddenly she doubts everything she's been doing. And Nick? The rest of the period he makes a point of disrupting.

What went wrong?

The teacher praised Nick in a way that he couldn't possibly accept.

> How you praise difficult students is as important as the fact that you do praise them.

Keep these guidelines in mind when you give praise and positive support to a difficult student.

 ## How to Praise Students Who Need Attention

At the elementary level, you can provide attention-seeking students positive attention openly and in front of their peers. Why? At this age, children are not embarassed by your public adulations. They like it! It gives them even more attention. And the added attention you give them by openly praising them helps fulfill their need for attention.

> Gerardo is a fourth-grade attention-seeking student who has had a lot of difficulty staying on task during group time. His teacher has taught him the behaviors she expects and has set goals for herself to give support when he behaves appropriately.
>
> Consequently, during class when she is seated and working with another group, she looks over and notices that Gerardo is working cooperatively with his own group. She stops what she is doing for a moment and says "Gerardo, good job. Your group is doing great, and you're really helping them!"

Middle and secondary attention-seeking students still want your attention, but in consideration of their age and the affect of peer responses, you need to provide praise quietly and one-to-one. You can praise these students by standing next to them in class and giving a more private positive message praising them for their efforts.

As tenth-grader Linda works quietly on her report, the teacher walks over to her desk, puts his hand on Linda's shoulder and says, "You're making wonderful progress on your report, Linda. Keep up the good work!"

For attention-seeking students of all ages:

- Tie your praise to a specific behavior.
- Give praise immediately.

How to Praise Students Who Need Limits

A student who needs to be tough, or in control, does not want to seem to be a "goody-goody" in front of his or her peers. Consequently, you do not want to give this student postive support in front of the entire class.

When you want to communicate praise to a student who needs limits, try these more subtle one-to-one approaches instead:

- Write a note on the student's homework before you hand it back.
- Write a brief note to the student and quietly place it on his or her desk.
- Make eye contact and give a nod.
- Give a quick thumbs up or a smile.
- Give verbal praise quietly and discreetly during or after class.

Giving praise to a student who needs limits can be tricky. If you're too enthusiastic or too public your praise can backfire and be rejected. Keep these precautions in mind:

• Be careful not to give praise too soon.
This student does not want to appear to be working to please you, so delay your recognition a bit. A casual thumbs up a few minutes later will get your message across.

• Always approach the student in a low-keyed manner.

This is not a student who will appreciate enthusiastic, effusive gushes of praise.

• Give consideration to age when choosing what you will say.

The younger the student, the more explicit you can be in your praise. Be less explicit and more casual and general with older students.

Here's how a teacher might praise a limit-seeking student for entering the classroom appropriately:

> Second-grade student:
>
> > "Jason, good job entering the classroom."
>
> Eighth-grade student:
>
> > "Phil, keep it up."

• Be wary of touching the student or making any other physical contact.

These are not the students who usually respond well to a pat on the back or a hand on the shoulder. Know your student before you make physical contact. Also, know your own district's policies. In some districts teachers may not touch students.

• Make "you" statements rather than "I" statements.

A limit-seeking student does not want your approval—it suggests that he or she is under your control. So instead of saying "I like the way you've started reading," simply nod and quietly say, "Your book's open, good." or "You're ready to read."

Why take these precautions when offering praise and positive support to limit-seeking students? Because they don't want the attention. They don't want anything that undermines their need to be in control, the tough guy, the leader. Given appropriately, however, your praise *will* have an effect.

Here's an example of a teacher praising a student who needs limits:

> Fifth-grader Jack has had a lot of trouble transitioning from one activity to another without pushing other students or responding defiantly to the teacher's directions. As a result, his teacher has been working with him to improve this behavior.
>
> Consequently, when Jack moved from his own seat to a group activity quietly, without bothering anyone, she wanted to be sure he knew that she was aware of the good behavioral choice he made.
>
> She also wanted to make sure that she did not call attention to Jack.
>
> A few minutes after the groups were involved in their assignment, she caught his eye, gave a nod and a quick thumbs up. Jack didn't smile or respond, but she knew he got the message.

 ## How to Praise Students Who Need Motivation

The key to praising students who need motivation is to always connect your positive support to their academic efforts. These students need constant encouragement to keep their enthusiasm high. Speak to the student one-to-one and let him or her know that you applaud the work accomplished, and that you have confidence that he or she can continue to do well.

Here's an example of a teacher praising a student who needs motivation:

> Natalie's teacher has to struggle to get Natalie to take even the first step on any assignment. Her self-confidence is so low that even the easiest assignment seems overwhelming to her. To help Natalie experience success,

the teacher breaks her work down into small increments. And then he makes sure that he praises Natalie each and every time these increments are completed.

Teacher: That's excellent, Natalie. Do you see what you've done? You've shown me that you can do these three long-division problems. They are all correct! And you know what? If you can do these three, you can do the next group. That's just great! I knew you could do it!

Positive Notes and Phone Calls

A personal note from you to a student can have a powerful impact. It shows you took the time and interest to recognize something he or she did. In your communication, focus on the student's successes, not on the failures. Positive notes and phone calls to difficult students should be used consistently throughout the year.

Here's an example of a positive note:

> Dear Cecilia,
>
> Just a note to let you know what a great job you did on your Civil War timeline. Your artwork is beautiful. You really are talented! I hope you'll allow me to keep it up in the room for awhile. It will help all of us while we're studying this unit.
>
> *Mrs. Smith*

Notes written on returned papers are also an effective way to get your message across.

Here's what a positive phone call might sound like:

> "Leon? This is Mr. Smith. I wanted to give you a quick call tonight to say that I am so pleased with the oral report you gave in class today. Your facts were straight, it was interesting to listen to and the photographs you showed made the whole presentation come to life.
>
> "I know you put a lot of work into it. Great job!"

Who wouldn't feel good receiving positive remarks like these?

Special Privileges

Special privileges are powerful reinforcers because they can be individualized to match a difficult student's interests and talents.

Your positive relationship with the student will help you determine the privileges that will be most reinforcing to him or her. The better you know your student, the better able you will be to choose privileges that are meaningful to the student.

> Note: Make sure the student is able to successfully handle the special privilege you give. For example, don't let a student who needs constant supervision run errands outside the classroom for you.

Here are some suggestions for special privileges:

Elementary	Secondary
• Be class monitor	• Receive extra computer time
• Care for class pet	• Sit by friend for one period
• Choose game for class	• Take one problem off a test
• Sit at teacher's desk	• Listen to music on headset
• Be first in line	• Create artwork to be displayed in class

Behavior Awards

Difficult students, particularly those who need attention, will appreciate the personal recognition and permanent record that are signified by a behavior award. These students will receive attention from you *and* attention from parents when the award is taken home. For maximum impact, be sure that the award notes the specific reason the student is being recognized. General recognition is not nearly as effective as specific recognition.

Tangible Rewards

Tangible rewards can be very reinforcing to difficult students who need the immediate gratification that a material reinforcement can bring. Some difficult students are not accustomed to receiving praise or special privileges and may be uncomfortable receiving them. A tangible reward may hold far more interest, at least until you have built a positive relationship that will make your praise meaningful and accessible to the student.

Tangible rewards include:

- Stickers
- Bookmarks
- Puzzles

- School supplies
- Colored pens
- Decals

- Books
- Magazines
- Art supplies

Peer Pressure

Your praise alone may not be enough to motivate a difficult student to choose appropriate behavior. You may need reinforcements—others who can add their encouragement to the positive support you provide. Where can you find this help? Look to your class. Each and every one of your students has the ability to encourage a difficult student to be a more responsible part of the class.

Peer pressure is one of the most effective tools a teacher can use to motivate a difficult student to choose appropriate behavior. You can take advantage of peer pressure through a classwide motivation system.

Here's how a classwide motivation system works:

1 Offer your students a classwide reward for good behavior, for example, a party at the end of the week, free time on Friday, or a half hour of music. (The reward, of course, should be age appropriate.)

2 Explain to your students that for everyone to receive the reward they will need to earn, as a class, (for example) 50 points.

3 To earn points, tell students that anytime you spot *any one of them* engaging in appropriate behavior, following directions or following the rules of the classroom, you will give the whole class a point. This <u>does not</u> mean the entire class has to be following the rules. It means that you will recognize one student for following the rules.

4   Designate a spot on the chalkboard as a scorekeeping area. Throughout the day, as you spot different students being good, award a point with some words of praise:

> "Jimmy has opened his book and has started reading. Good work, Jimmy. That's a point for the class toward the party on Friday."

How does this system specifically benefit your difficult students?

More motivation to choose appropriate behavior! If, for example, you have set a goal to give positive support to a specific student ten times a day, turn those recognitions into classwide points and the positive effects will be doubled. The student receives praise and recognition from you, and the class moves closer to a reward, which earns recognition from them. The difficult student will be even more motivated to comply.

Also, by making sure that your difficult students are earning many of the classwide points you can really use this system as an individualized approach for recognizing these students.

> Keep in mind also that your own words of recognition and praise when you award a point to a difficult student should be geared toward the student's primary need. Look back at pages 103-108 for guidelines.

Here's an example of a fifth-grade teacher introducing a classwide motivation system to her class:

Teacher: Okay, class. I've got a great idea I'd like to introduce. And this is one idea I know you'll like! But first, who can tell me the rules of our classroom?

Hands raise.

Teacher: Rob?

Rob: Follow directions. Keep hands, feet and objects to yourself. Ask permission before getting out of seat.

Teacher: That's right. We've been talking a lot recently about these rules. Now I've got an idea that will help encourage everyone to follow these rules.

Here it is:

We're all going to work toward earning a special privilege. From discussions we've had, I know that you'd all like to have a classroom party with music. Here's a way to earn that party. I'm going to be looking for students who are following the rules. During the day, when I see a student following the rules I'll put a point on the board. For example, if it's time to move into groups for social studies and I see Jessica pick up her books and quietly go to her seat, I might say, "Jessica's following directions for going to group. That's a point for the class." Then I'll add a point to the board.

There's no limit to how many points you all can earn during a day. When you get to 50 points you'll earn the party!

Any questions?

Here's how this system will benefit each type of special need.

 Students Who Need Attention

These students love attention, so they'll particularly like being a visible part of earning a reward the whole class wants. With a classwide motivation system, these students not only can earn attention from you but they get added attention from their peers. Every time they earn a point they'll help the class move ahead toward a reward.

For example:

> A third-grade class enters the room after lunch. Lisa, a student who is often disruptive at this time, enters appropriately. The teacher awards the class a point for Lisa's behavior.

> Teacher: Good job entering the room quietly, Lisa. That's a point for the class. We're that much closer to a half hour of free time on the yard Friday!

> Student: Way to go, Lisa!

> Student: Yeah, Lisa!

 Students Who Need Limits

These students may not want or even accept praise from you, but they may accept some adulation from the class. They may even enjoy the recognition and attention they get when they bring the class closer to its reward. A classwide system gives the student an opportunity to choose appropriate behavior not for you, but for the class—a much more agreeable, perhaps powerful position. It puts the student in the leadership role—the control role—that he or she wants. And the student is using appropriate behavior to do so.

For example:

> A sixth-grade class is listening to a directed social studies lesson. Chris, a student who is usually confrontational and disruptive, raises his hand to answer a question. After he gives his answer, the teacher adds:
>
> Teacher: Chris raised his hand. (*She adds a point to the board.*) Now we're another point closer to a half hour of music on Friday.
>
> Another student looks at Chris and nods. A girl who sits behind Chris taps his shoulder and says, "All right!"

◼ Students Who Need Motivation

Having the whole class cheering them on can greatly boost their motivation to succeed. Whenever you see this child working, add a point to the board! The whole class will be appreciative and let the point-winning student know it.

> A seventh-grade teacher has directed the class to answer a series of questions in their history book. Seeing that Patty, a student who needs motivation, has completed one question and is starting on the second, the teacher moves to the board, adds a point, and says:
>
> Teacher: Patty's getting a great start. That's a point for the whole class.
>
> Students: (*break into brief applause*)

When giving positive recognition keep these guidelines in mind:

Prompt reinforcement is effective reinforcement.

Be sure to give the reward immediately after you have observed the desired behavior. You want the student to associate this behavior with the reward, and the longer you wait, the less effective the reinforcer will be.

Pair positives with praise.

Whenever you give a student a tangible reward, a special privilege or a behavior award, always pair it with meaningful, specific praise such as "Here's a sticker for coming into the classroom so quietly, Jess." Don't assume that a student always knows why he or she is being recognized.

Because you want the behavior to be repeated, be specific.

Keep building the positive relationship.

Every time you reinforce a student you have a great opportunity to build the positive relationship even further. Make the most of this opportunity by communicating your pride, enthusiasm and caring through the way you speak and the way you interact as you deliver the recognition.

Redirecting Nondisruptive Off-Task Behavior

"I know Michelle isn't really doing her work, but she doesn't bother anyone, either. She just stares out the window or looks off into space. Of course, for all the attention she pays she might as well not even be sitting in class."

There are two types of inappropriate classroom behavior that hinder a student's success in school: disruptive behavior and nondisruptive off-task behavior.

> With difficult students it is especially important to differentiate between the two because each is best handled through very different responses.

Disruptive behavior is obvious. It's overt misbehavior that keeps you from teaching and keeps other students from learning. Disruptive behaviors include talking back, arguing, tantrums, fighting, making noises or openly refusing to work.

Nondisruptive off-task behavior is far more subtle. It's behavior that is off task but is not disturbing others—for example, staring out of the window, not doing assigned work, doodling, putting head down on desk or doing something other than the assigned task. The student does nothing to cause a disturbance, but you can clearly see he or she is not paying attention, is not part of the class and isn't participating.

What happens when students are nondisruptive but off task?

Teachers typically react to this behavior in one of two reactive ways:

- They ignore the behavior, or
- they immediately give a consequence.

Both of these responses are not in the student's best interest. Here's why:

Ignoring nondisruptive off-task behavior

> As she is leading a class discussion, a teacher sees that Carolyn has put her head down on the table and has closed her eyes. Because Carolyn is a disruptive, confrontational student, and the teacher is in no mood today for dealing with her abusive behavior, she says nothing and Carolyn spends the rest of the period asleep.

When you simply ignore a difficult student's nondisruptive off-task behavior you may think you're making things easier on yourself (no confrontations, no defiant responses, no arguments), but you send this message to the student:

> "In my class it's okay if you don't participate, if you tune me out and ultimately fail. That's all right as long as you don't bother anyone else."

What does that say to the student?

> "My expectations for you are so low that it really doesn't matter if you're part of this class or not. I expect other kids to stay on task. I don't expect it of you. As long as you don't bother me I won't bother you. Have we got a deal?"

These are probably familiar messages to difficult students. After all, they're used to being written off. Messages such as these will do nothing to raise a student's self-esteem or motivate him or her to change behavior. And, in the long run, allowing a student to fail will do nothing for your self-esteem either.

Ignoring a student's nondisruptive off-task behavior will not help this student succeed. After all, no action has been taken to get the student back on task. And ignoring a student's nondisruptive off-task behavior will never help you build a more positive relationship with the student.

There's no caring message in this response.

Giving an immediate consequence

> A teacher is presenting a lesson to the class. As he looks around the room he notices that Marco has stopped paying attention and is looking out the window. What is his response? He anxiously reacts to the off-task behavior and does the first thing that comes to his mind to put an end to it. "Marco, eyes up front! That's detention for you today!"

Giving an immediate consequence to a nondisruptive off-task student is a reactive response that often sends an unnecessarily harsh, punitive message. It's easy for anyone, especially a difficult student, to experience a lapse of attention. If the off-task behavior is nondisruptive, proactive teachers plan to first give the student an opportunity to get back on task *before* taking further, more serious corrective actions.

Negative consequences should only be used as a last resort in responding to this behavior. Providing a consequence when a lesser action will do the job will only further alienate an already alienated student.

How should you deal with nondisruptive off-task behavior?

As we have been emphasizing in this book, teachers who are successful with difficult students try their best to use every opportunity available to build up their relationship with these students. Nondisruptive off-task behavior provides such an opportunity.

It provides the opportunity to say to a student, "Your behavior is inappropriate, but I care about you and I'm going to give you the chance to choose more appropriate behavior."

What a vote of confidence! What a demonstration of high expectations!

What can you do?

> Give nondisruptive off-task students the opportunity to meet your expectations by redirecting their behavior.

On the following pages you will find a variety of redirecting techniques you can use to help an off-task student get back on task. Once again, you will notice that these techniques have been individualized to meet a difficult student's primary needs.

 ### Redirecting Students Who Need Attention

Students who need attention are usually the easiest to redirect back on task. After all, these students want your attention. By giving that attention in a redirecting manner you'll be meeting their needs and positively guiding them toward better behavior choices at the same time.

Try these techniques with attention-seeking students:

Redirecting Technique: The Look

> Instead of listening to a directed lesson, sixth-grader Kenny sits rocking back and forth in his seat, his eyes wandering the room. When the teacher notices his behavior, she makes direct eye contact and looks at him with a firm, calm expression on her face. She maintains this eye contact until Kenny puts all four legs of his chair on the floor and begins to pay attention.

When a student stares off into space or gazes out the window, just catch his eye and give him a look—a purposeful, meaningful look that says, "I've noticed your behavior, I disapprove, and I want you to get back on task now!" Then hold that look until he gets back on task.

No words are spoken, yet the message is clear. And often it's enough to motivate the student to start paying attention. No need for consequences. No need for the student to stay off task.

Redirecting Technique: Physical Proximity

> While reading a newspaper article to the class, the teacher notices that Danielle has put her head down on her desk and has tuned out. Continuing to read, the teacher walks back to Danielle's desk and stands near her while she continues reading the article. Danielle quickly notices her presence, lifts her head and starts paying attention.

When you notice a student has fallen off task, just walk over and stand by his or her desk. You may tap the student on the shoulder, or you may just stand there. Either way, the message (and your attention) will be communicated.

Redirecting Technique: Mention the Student's Name

> While presenting a math lesson at the board, the teacher
> sees that Rosa is off task and doodling on her paper
> instead of following along. The teacher, in a matter-of-fact
> manner, continues the lesson saying, "I want all of you,
> including Rosa, to come up with the answer to this
> problem." As soon as she hears her name mentioned, Rosa
> gets back on task.

When a student is falling off-task, simply wake her up a bit by including her name in your lesson.

These techniques all provide ways of bringing the attention-seeking student back on task without having to turn to consequences. The student is part of the classroom again, his or her need for attention is recognized, and you have taken more steps to further build a positive relationship.

You've shown that you care enough to do more than hand out a consequence. You care enough to guide the student toward more responsible behavior.

Redirecting Students Who Need Limits

Now, what about tougher, more confrontational students? These students *don't* want your attention. How can redirecting work with them? It can work very effectively if it is delivered quietly without drawing a lot of attention to the student. Here are some suggestions:

Redirecting Technique: Seat the Student by You

Evan is a tough kid who can usually be counted on to be off task in class. Knowing this, his teacher has prepared by seating him at the front of the room near her desk. When Evan loses interest and puts his head down on his desk, or tunes out, she is able to very quietly, without calling attention to either herself or to Evan, give him a tap on the shoulder or a look that prompts him to get back on task. Her actions are so subtle, so nonconfrontational, that Evan is able to accept her prompt.

Many teachers seat their confrontational students as far away from them as possible, but the closer they are seated to you, the easier it will be for you to guide them toward better behavioral choices *and* build a relationship with them. Close by, your interactions can be more discreet, less obvious to the rest of the students. This allows your students to save face, which lessens resistance to you and your efforts.

Redirecting Technique: Physical Proximity

As with the student who needs attention, standing by a student who needs firm limits may be sufficient to motivate him or her back on task. By proactively planning to be there, you can deter these students' tendencies to go off task. You can stay on top of the situation and nip inappropriate behavior in the bud.

Redirecting Technique: Remind the Student about the Rules

John is a difficult student who will seize upon any opportunity to get off task. Transitions are a particularly tough time for him. Knowing this, as the class is about to transition to another activity, the teacher walks quietly over to John and says, "Remember, John, take your book, walk straight to your social studies group and sit down, no talking." After this brief reminder, the teacher walks on. No fuss. No big deal.

Reminding a student of the directions he or she is to follow is an excellent proactive technique to use with a student who needs limits.

■ Redirecting Students Who Need Motivation

These students need massive amounts of motivation and encouragement. As a result, redirecting by itself may be too subtle to be effective in getting them on task. They need more than a nudge.

> Keep this in mind: With difficult students, nondisruptive off-task behavior is often a precursor to more disruptive behaviors. By redirecting the behavior in an appropriate direction you will lessen the likelihood of it escalating and therefore lessen the likelihood of having to use additional consequences.

And remember to be positive! When a nondisruptive off-task student is redirected back on task don't let it go at that. Give plenty of positive support for the appropriate behavior choice the student has made. As always, provide that support in a manner that fits the student's needs.

"Good job listening, Greg."

Decreasing Disruptive
Behavior

"I feel sorry and concerned about the trouble
Steven has had to deal with in his life, but I cannot
let him run my room. Nobody else seems to have
ever set limits for him, but someone had better do it
soon or this child won't ever have a chance to
succeed."

With some students it will be inevitable.

No matter how proactively you've taught and reminded a difficult
student of the behavior you expect, and no matter how consistent you've
been in reinforcing the behavior, there are still going to be times when a
difficult student will continue to disrupt.

Remember, these are tough students. They're below the Trust Line for a
reason. Interactions with teachers have been negative. School has not
been a positive experience for them. These students won't always care
about your positive support.

So in spite of all the steps you've taken to this point with a difficult
student, there will still be times when he or she will continue to talk back,
will continue to refuse to work, or continue to engage in other
unacceptable behaviors. There will be times when this student will still
stop you from teaching and other students from learning.

When this happens you'll have to use corrective actions to get the student back on task.

Remember, a difficult student must be held accountable to the same behavioral limits as your other students. The student's eventual success will depend upon a balance between the positive relationship you are building by reaching out to him or her and the limits you set and enforce.

Using corrective actions is one of the greatest challenges you'll face in dealing with difficult students. After all, these students are used to intimidating teachers into backing down on their limits. They are accustomed to ignoring your guidance.

In this chapter you will learn how to proactively plan what you will do when disruptions occur. You will learn how to use consequences effectively and in a manner that best meets a student's specific needs.

Before we begin, a few words about consequences . . .

- The goal of the consequences you provide a difficult student should be to stop the unacceptable behavior and to help the student make better choices or learn a new behavior. Consequences are not meant to punish a student.

- It is not the severity of the consequence that matters. It is the consistency with which it is implemented. Difficult students require more structure than other students. They must absolutely understand that every time they choose to disrupt, you will intervene and take action. Minimal consequences are often the most effective because you are likely to use them consistently.

- When appropriate, the consequence should be given immediately or as soon as possible after the disruption. Your goal is to teach acceptable behavior. A consequence given hours after the fact will not be as effective as one that can be provided sooner.

With these guidelines in mind, we will look at two different ways to use consequences in your classroom:

1) A teacher-selected hierarchy of consequences

2) A teacher/student selected hierarchy of consequences ("You Pick. We Pick. I Pick.")

Discipline Hierarchy
Teacher-Selected Hierarchy of Consequences

Many teachers use consequences within the context of a discipline hierarchy that is part of a general classroom discipline plan.

> A classroom discipline plan is a behavior management system that allows you to spell out the behavior you expect from all students and what they can expect from you in return. This plan provides an extremely effective framework around which all of your classroom management efforts can be organized.

A classroom discipline plan consists of three parts:

Rules that all students must follow at all times.

Positive Recognition that students will receive for following the rules.

Consequences that result when students choose not to follow the rules.

Sample Classroom Discipline Plan

Classroom Rules

Follow directions.

Keep hands, feet and objects to yourself.

No swearing, teasing or name calling.

Positive Recognition

Praise

Positive notes sent home to parents

Select own seat for the day

Consequences (Discipline Hierarchy)

First time student breaks a rule:	Warning
Second time:	Stay in class 1 minute after the bell.
Third time:	Stay in class 2 minutes after bell.
Fourth time:	Teacher calls parents.
Fifth time:	Send to principal.

Severe Clause (for major infraction): Send to principal.

It is not uncommon to find that excessive disruptive behavior within one class is caused not by a large number of difficult students, but rather by problems in the overall behavior management of the class.

For this reason, it is appropriate to focus briefly on the value of a well-defined classroom discipline plan not only in the context of using consequences, but as the foundation of a smoothly running, effective and motivating classroom as well.

Teachers often find that having such a plan in place can greatly minimize disruptive behavior in their classroom.

Benefits of a Classroom Discipline Plan for All Students

A classroom discipline plan is beneficial for you and beneficial for all of your students. Here's why:

• A discipline plan makes managing student behavior easier.

As emphasized in Section One of this book, planning is the key to any successful classroom management effort. When you have a plan for how you will respond to student behavior you won't have to make on-the-spot decisions about what to do when a student misbehaves—or how to properly recognize a student who does behave appropriately. You'll know what to do, your students will know what to expect, and the guesswork (and a lot of stress) will be eliminated from your daily disciplinary efforts. Your responses to discipline problems can be calm, assured and confident. A classroom discipline plan is an essential part of being able to respond proactively to students.

• A discipline plan protects students' rights.

All students have the right to the same due process in the classroom. A discipline plan will help ensure that you deal with each student in a fair and consistent manner.

• A discipline plan helps ensure safety for all students in the classroom.

Consistently used as part of a teacher's behavior management efforts, a classroom discipline plan helps reduce behavior problems in class. And reduced behavior problems mean a safer environment for all students.

• A discipline plan helps ensure parental support.

When you communicate your discipline plan to parents you are letting them know that you care about guiding their children toward making responsible behavioral choices. This is a powerful message of support and professionalism to give to parents.

• A discipline plan helps ensure administrator support.

A discipline plan demonstrates to your administrator (dean, counselor, principal or vice principal) that you have a well thought-out course of action for managing student behavior in your classroom. When your administrator understands the commitment you've made to effective classroom management, you will be better able to get support when you need it.

Benefits of a Classroom Discipline Plan for Difficult Students

A discipline plan will help any classroom function better. All students benefit from the structure of clearly stated classroom rules, positive recognition and consequences.

A discipline plan is critical, however, for difficult students.

The trust that allows most of your students to generally choose responsible, compliant behavior is missing with difficult students. They need the structure and the consistency that a classroom discipline plan provides. And they need it every day, all day long.

To be this consistent you need a structured plan to help you proactively know what you will do when misbehavior occurs. Without a structured plan it's almost inevitable that you will fall into the reactive, inconsistent responses that tear down, rather than build up, positive relationships.

• Difficult students need clearly defined rules.

If difficult students are to succeed in your classroom, they need to know exactly what is expected of them. No guessing. No assumptions. No vague expectations. If they are to be held accountable to rules (as they must be), those rules have to be made crystal clear. And because these students are accustomed to being singled out, it is important that they see that *the same rules are in place for everyone*. General classroom rules are an important equalizing force in a classroom.

> As the difficult student's teacher, you too need to know exactly what expectations your students are accountable to. Otherwise you have no clear behavioral basis upon which to provide both the positive recognition and consequences these students need.

• Difficult students need consistent positive recognition.

As has been emphasized, none of your behavior management efforts will mean anything to a difficult student unless you are building a positive relationship at the same time. For this reason, positive support is a vital part of a classroom discipline plan. Difficult students need to know that their responsible choices will be recognized.

> When positive support is built into your daily classroom management routine, you will find that building a positive relationship with a difficult student (and all students) becomes a far more natural, and consistent, part of each day.

• Difficult students need consistently applied, appropriate consequences.

Difficult students are accustomed to being written off, ignored, severely punished, or inconsistently held accountable. They need to know that you care enough about them to set limits and to stick to those limits.

> As the difficult student's teacher, you need a clear plan for how you will respond to the student's misbehavior. Without such a plan you will inevitably react from emotion, not from a proactive stance.

The point is this: In terms of behavior management you can have an off day with most of your students. If you are sporadic in your use of positive recognition, the majority of students will still be compliant— they'll do their work and they will be back in class the next day.

If your consequences are not particularly meaningful, or are given inconsistently, most of your students will still probably behave appropriately because they don't want to get into trouble.

With difficult students there is no margin for error.

With difficult students, however, you can't leave anything to chance. There is no margin for error here. An off day with a difficult student can result in significant setbacks. Not only is the opportunity for building the relationship lost, but in addition the student falls further below the Trust Line. An off day with a difficult student is detrimental to everything you want to accomplish with this student.

A classroom discipline plan will help you minimize off days and, most of all, maximize your positive relationship with the difficult student.

Using a Discipline Hierarchy as Part of a Classroom Plan

A discipline hierarchy lists consequences in the order in which they will be imposed for noncompliant behavior (breaking classroom rules) within a day or within a class period. The hierarchy is progressive, starting with a warning the first time a student breaks a rule. The consequences then become gradually more substantial for the second, third, fourth and fifth time that a student disrupts in a day or class period.

For example:

Sample Discipline Hierarchy for Grades 4-6

First time a student breaks a rule:	Warning
Second time:	10 minutes working away from the group
Third time:	15 minutes working away from the group
Fourth time:	Call parents
Fifth time:	Send to principal
Major Infraction:	(Severe Clause) Send immediately to principal

A finite set of consequences such as this is important for a well-managed classroom. The students will understand exactly what will happen each time they misbehave. This gives them a sense of security in understanding the parameters of how the teacher will respond. This hierarchy of consequences also gives the teacher a sense of security because he or she knows how to respond to misbehavior without worrying about being unfair or reactive.

If you already have a discipline hierarchy in place as part of a classroom discipline plan, stop and evaluate it. If you have a large number of difficult students you may choose to either change the consequences (see suggested consequences on pages 144-150) or change the way you implement the hierarchy.

When hierarchies are not working with difficult students it is often due to the following reasons:

• Teachers often give negative consequences when they really aren't needed.

Teachers have a natural tendency, especially with difficult students, to look for negative behavior. When they find it, they tend to jump on it—to do something quickly to stop it. To lessen their anxiety, one of the most common mistakes teachers make in implementing a hierarchy with difficult students is giving consequences when lesser, more positive steps *might have been taken first*. As we stressed in Chapter 7, proactive use of positive recognition can often eliminate or delay the need for consequences. And in Chapter 8 you learned that redirecting can often get a nondisruptive student back on task without the need to turn to stronger measures.

The difficult student needs a trusting, positive relationship with you just as much as he or she needs to be held accountable. If, when appropriate, you can achieve both of these objectives through means other than consequences, you've taken one more step in moving the student back up toward the Trust Line.

• Teachers often give consequences that are too severe or too inconvenient to enforce.

If one of your consequences is having a student stay 15 or 30 minutes after school, you may find that your student isn't the only one who doesn't want to stay. You may not want to stay, either. In fact, maybe you *can't* stay—you've got a faculty meeting right after class! What happens then?

Teachers who give consequences that are too severe or inconvenient inevitably begin to issue consequences inconsistently.

With difficult students, there can be no inconsistency. They need structure—clearly defined behavioral parameters. Students need to know that consequences are real results of choices they make. Inconsistency only reinforces their mistaken belief that they can do what they choose to do, and it's only by chance or bad luck that anything negative will come of it at all.

• Teachers continue to use consequences that are ineffective.
Should you find yourself giving the same consequences over and over again, it's time to evaluate those consequences. If they are not helping teach students to choose more appropriate behavior, you need to find out why.

- Are the consequences so inconvenient that you are not giving them consistently?

- Are the consequences not enough of a deterrent to matter to the student?

- Are the consequences so severe that the student reacts with increased anger and hostility?

> Remember, the goal in giving a consequence is to help a student make better behavior choices. Make sure the consequences contained in your discipline hierarchy will guide your student to do that.

Suggested consequences can be found on pages 144-150.

If you already have a discipline hierarchy in place, and you are satisfied that the consequences listed are appropriate, you will need to focus on individualizing the way you provide these consequences to your difficult students. On pages 150-153 you will find guidelines for implementing consequences according to a student's specific needs.

> Important: If you already have a discipline hierarchy in effect in your classroom, your difficult students should be held accountable to this hierarchy.

If you do not have a discipline hierarchy in place:

Here are guidelines for developing a discipline hierarchy. Although you can create a hierarchy for a single student, ideally, it should be in place for the entire class as part of a fully developed classroom discipline plan. It's easier for you to implement and it demonstrates to your difficult students that they are accountable to the same expectations as are other students.

• First Time a Student Disrupts

Most teachers issue a warning the first time a student disrupts or breaks a rule of the classroom.

> "Corey, the direction was to work without talking. That's a warning."

> "Gary, the rule in this classroom is no swearing. That's a warning."

A warning gives the student an opportunity to choose more appropriate behavior before a more substantial consequence is received. It is a powerful reminder, one that carries an important message. The student knows that the next disruption will bring with it a real consequence.

• Second Time a Student Disrupts

The second or third time a student disrupts in the same day, or the same period, the teacher needs to provide a consequence. These consequences must be easy to implement, and not time consuming. Typical consequences for second or third infractions include time out, one-minute wait after class, and filling out a Think Sheet. (The Think Sheet is explained on page 146.)

• Fourth Time a Student Disrupts

You need to **contact parents** if a student disrupts a fourth time in a day (self-contained classrooms) or in a class period (upper grades). Parent contact is a key component of managing student behavior. For some students, involving parents will be the only way you will motivate them toward appropriate behavior. Teachers typically give the parent a call or send a note home to let the parent know that a student's behavior is disruptive and cannot continue. Students need to know that you will be consistent in the enforcement of this consequence. And parents need to know where they fit in.

• Fifth Time a Student Disrupts

Sending a student to the principal or vice principal should be the last consequence on a discipline hierarchy. In preparation for implementing this consequence, you must have already met with your administrator to discuss actions he or she will take when students are sent to the office. You need to know that the administrator will provide the help and support you need. The administrator's role might include counseling with the student, conferencing with the parents or suspending a severely disruptive student.

• Severe Clause

In cases of severe misbehavior, such as fighting, vandalism, defying a teacher or in some way stopping the entire class from functioning, a student would not receive a warning. He or she loses the right to proceed through the hierarchy of consequences. Severe misbehavior calls for an immediate consequence that will remove the student from the classroom.

On a discipline hierarchy this is called a Severe Clause.

Sample Discipline Hierarchy for Grades K-3

First time a student breaks a rule:	Warning
Second time:	5 minutes working away from the group
Third time:	10 minutes working away from the group
Fourth time:	Call parents
Fifth time:	Send to principal
Severe Clause:	Send to principal

Sample Discipline Hierarchy for Grades 4-6

First time a student breaks a rule:	Warning
Second time:	10 minutes working away from the group
Third time:	15 minutes working away from the group plus fill out a Think Sheet
Fourth time:	Call parents
Fifth time:	Send to principal
Severe Clause:	Send to principal

Sample Discipline Hierarchy for Grades 7-12

First time student breaks a rule:	Warning
Second time:	Stay in class 1 minute after the bell
Third time:	Stay in class 2 minutes after the bell plus fill out a Think Sheet
Fourth time:	Call parents
Fifth time:	Send to administrator
Severe Clause:	Send to administrator

A discipline hierarchy is a very effective way to use consequences with all of your students. The value of a hierarchy is that everyone—you, students and parents—will know exactly what will happen each time misbehavior occurs. No surprises. No unequal treatment.

For complete guidelines for developing and implementing a discipline hierarchy as part of a complete classroom discipline plan, please see Lee Canter's revised *Assertive Discipline–Positive Behavior Management for Today's Classroom.*

Dropping Down on a Discipline Hierarchy

You may find that a difficult student does not respond to the basic consequences used in your general discipline hierarchy. A warning, a one-minute or two-minute wait after class or time out—consequences that are effective for most of your students—just may not be sufficient to motivate this student to choose to behave responsibly.

When this happens you can adjust your discipline hierarchy to better meet the student's needs.

Here's how:

Often you will find the difficult student reaches the same consequence on the hierarchy each day. For example, each day a student might reach the third step on the hierarchy (see example below) and stay after class for two minutes. It would appear in this case that the student does not really mind staying after class and thus the consequence is not effective.

First disruption:	Warning
Second disruption:	One minute after class
Third disruption:	**Two minutes after class**
Fourth disruption:	Contact parents
Fifth disruption:	Send student to principal

It is important to note, however, that this student always stops short of the consequence that involves calling the parent. In this case the teacher can conclude that it may be effective to change this student's discipline hierarchy so that the first time she disrupts, instead of a warning, instead of staying after class, her parents are immediately contacted.

The discipline hierarchy for this student then becomes as follows:

First disruption:	Call parents
Second disruption:	Send student to principal

Once improvement is seen and sustained, the student may return to the discipline hierarchy that is in place for the rest of the class.

You Pick. We Pick. I Pick.
Teacher/Student-Selected Hierarchy of Consequences

Some difficult students, especially those who are confrontational and are in a power struggle with you, can be extremely resentful of consequences they feel are arbitrarily imposed on them. This resentment can be so intense that it actually hinders their ability to respond to your consequences.

These students may be far more receptive to your discipline efforts if they are involved in selecting the consequences that will be imposed for misbehavior. The more they are involved, the better the chance that these "power" students will buy into your plan and accept responsibility for their actions.

Here's how to use the "You Pick. We Pick. I Pick." system:

1. Develop a list of appropriate consequences that range from very mild to more serious. (Refer to the suggested consequences on pages 144 150 for ideas.)

For example:

Sample Elementary List	Sample Middle/Secondary List
• Ten minutes time out • Miss recess • Time out in another class • Student calls parent • Teacher calls parent	• One minute after class • Two minutes after class plus Think Sheet • Student writes a letter home • Student calls parent • Teacher calls parent

2. Meet with the student. Follow these guidelines as you explain how the plan works.

Explain rationale.

> Teacher: Alan, you've been having a lot of trouble making good choices in class. You've been pushing other students, talking out and making it hard for others to pay attention. You're also making it hard for yourself. I want you to be more successful in this class. I want to help you make better choices. So here's what we're going to do.

Show the list of consequences to the student. Then explain how the plan will work.

> Teacher: I have put together a list of consequences that I feel will help you make better choices about how to behave in class. Right now you are going to help me decide how we are going to use these consequences. You're going to have an opportunity to choose what will happen when you choose to misbehave.

The teacher first reads through the list of consequences with the student. She carefully explains each one and answers any questions he may have.

> Teacher: Okay, Alan. Do you understand what all of these consequences mean?

> Student: Sure.

> Teacher: Good. Now what do you think I should do the first time you make a poor choice and misbehave each day? Which of these consequences might help get you back on track? Look at the list and you pick. It's up to you. What do you think should happen the first time you misbehave?

The student looks over the list and chooses one consequence.

Teacher: All right. You've decided that the first time you break a rule you'll go to time out for 10 minutes. Is that right?

Student: Yeah, I guess.

Teacher: OK. That's a good choice. But if that doesn't work, Alan, and you misbehave a *second* time in a day there has to be a different consequence. This time we will both pick a consequence together. If we can't agree, I'll have to pick. Let's look at the list again.

Alan and the teacher look at the list and talk about the different consequences. They finally agree on missing recess.

Teacher: All right, Alan. We've agreed that the second time you misbehave in a day you will miss recess. Is that correct?

Student: Yeah.

Teacher: Good. You picked a consequence. We picked one together. Now it's my turn to pick. If time out and missing recess don't work, and you misbehave a *third* time, and I really hope this doesn't happen, I'm going to send to you to Mr. Murphy's room for one half hour. You'll take your assignments, go to his classroom, sit quietly and do your work. For one half hour.

Student: No way. I don't want to go to Mr. Murphy's room. It's not fair. None of the other kids ever have to.

Teacher: I understand, Alan, but I have to take more steps to help you. And remember, it's your choice.

> Teacher: Now, so that neither of us will forget what our
> plan is, let's write everything down and go over
> it once more. What will happen the first time you
> misbehave in a day . . .

By giving a student a more participatory role in the process, it is made even clearer that he or she is responsible for what will occur should misbehavior continue. The student is thus empowered to make decisions that directly effect him or her.

This system also allows you to provide consequences on a very individualized basis—consequences that will be most meaningful to the student.

> Keep in mind too that the collaborative nature of this system
> provides an opportunity to further build a positive relationship
> with this student.

If appropriate, you may also want to involve the student in a discussion regarding which consequences should be on the list.

Suggested Consequences

On the following pages you will find a selection of consequences that teachers have proven effective in their classrooms.

- Time Out
- One Minute After Class
- Tape Record a Student's Behavior
- Have Student Call Parent
- Write Letter Home
- Time Out in Another Class
- Think Sheet (in conjunction with another corrective action)

Time Out

> Instead of doing her assigned work, fourth-grader Lisa keeps turning around and bothering her neighbors, talking to them and pulling at their papers. She has received a warning, but the disruptive behavior has continued.
>
> In response, her teacher walks over to her and calmly tells her: "Lisa, I want you to take your worksheet and sit in the back of the room until I tell you to return to your seat."

One of the most effective corrective interventions for elementary students is to simply remove the student from the situation in which he or she is disrupting. During this time out, the student sits apart from the rest of the class, but is expected to continue to do work or listen to the lesson. If appropriate, a very disruptive difficult student can be seated close to you so you can easily monitor his or her behavior, give positive feedback or redirect behavior as needed.

The advantages to time out are twofold:

1. By removing the student from the situation in which he or she is disrupting, you immediately stop the disruptive behavior. The rest of the class can get back on task.

   > When Lisa is sitting by herself she won't be in a situation where she has an opportunity to talk to her neighbors or fool around with their papers. If, however, the consequence had been to stay after school for 10 minutes, Lisa still would continue to be by her neighbors and still have an opportunity to disrupt.

2. The student is given an opportunity to calm down and get back on task without the distraction of other students.

   > Seated by herself, Lisa is more likely to settle down and focus on her work. This is particularly helpful when a student is upset or angry.

Think Sheet

Your goal in providing a consequence is not to punish, but to stop misbehavior and keep it from escalating. A Think Sheet provides an excellent opportunity for an older student to stop and evaluate his or her inappropriate behavior and also to consider other behaviors that might be better choices in the future.

If age appropriate, when a student is disruptive or breaks a classroom rule have him or her write an account of the misbehavior during recess, after class or at home.

The Think Sheet should include the following points:

- The misbehavior or rule that was broken
- Why the student chose to misbehave
- Who was bothered (fellow students, teacher, etc.)
- What more appropriate behavior the student could choose next time

---

Think Sheet

Student's Name _____ Class/Period _____ Date _____

This is the rule I broke: _____

_____

I chose to break this rule because: _____

_____

_____

_____

_____

_____

_____

Who was bothered when I broke this rule? _____

_____

This is what I could have done instead: _____

_____

_____

_____

_____

_____

Student Signature _____ Date _____

The Think Sheet gives the student an opportunity to calmly think through his or her behavioral choices. The Think Sheet will also provide you a "student's point of view" forum from which to address a student's problem behavior in a one-to-one conference. We'll look further into this in Chapter 11.

> Note: The Think Sheet in and of itself is not a consequence, but should be given in conjunction with another corrective action such as time out or after-school detention. The act of filling out the Think Sheet helps to calm the student down and evaluate his or her behavior.

One Minute After Class

For middle or secondary students, one of the most effective corrective interventions is to keep the student after class for one minute.

> Remember, it isn't the severity of a consequence, it is the consistency with which it is used that makes it effective.

To an older student, one minute away from peers can seem like forever. Just one minute is enough to make a student miss walking to the next class with friends, be last in line at lunch or unable to join a group after school. Don't underestimate the power of this consequence for older students.

In this one minute, you also have an opportunity to briefly speak with the student about his or her behavior, work on the relationship and help the student make better behavior choices in the future.

> "Chris, the rule of this classroom is no swearing. If you swear in class, you will be choosing to remain after the other students have left, like today. Do you think there's anything you can do to remind yourself to use more appropriate behavior in class?"

The ease of use of this consequence increases the likelihood that you will be consistent in its use.

Tape Record a Student's Behavior

Difficult students, particularly those who need limits, are often highly manipulative and will try to convince parents that you are picking on them—that they are doing nothing wrong. Recording their behavior is an extremely effective technique to use.*

Here's how to use this consequence:

> When a student disrupts, place a cassette recorder next to him or her and press "record." Tell the student that the recorder will remain on for the rest of the day or period and that you will play the recorded tape for his or her parents and/or the administrator. By turning on the tape recorder, you are sending a strong message to the student that you will follow through. Most often, this technique stops the inappropriate behavior immediately.

*This consequence would not be appropriate as part of a general classroom discipline hierarchy that involves the entire class. It would, however, be highly effective when used on a more individualized basis, for instance as part of the "You Pick. We Pick. I Pick." system that is described on pages 141-144.

Have Student Call Parent

Requiring a student to explain his or her disruptive behavior to a parent can be an extremely strong deterrent.

Some teachers today have portable telephones in their classroom and have had great success in having a student call his or her parent immediately after the student has been disruptive. This phone call could take place at recess, at lunch or at the end of the period. Having a phone available and calling immediately communicates to the student that you are serious about setting limits.

If a phone is not available in your classroom, the student needs to call as soon as both of you can get to a phone in the building.

Have Student Write a Letter Home

Writing a letter home explaining misbehavior can also be an effective consequence, particularly for older students. In the letter, the student simply explains to the parent how he or she misbehaved. Caution: Do not use this consequence if you have suspicions that a parent might respond with hostility and harm the child.

Time Out in Another Classroom

When a student is highly disruptive, it may be useful to send him or her to another classroom. When the student is in a power struggle with you, he or she may not act up in another teacher's classroom. There are several guidelines you must follow when using time out in another classroom:

- Send the student to a well-run classroom.

- The student should be sent to the same or a higher grade level. The student should not be sent to a much lower grade level because it would be considered humiliating.

- The student should stay for a limited amount of time, do academic work or possibly fill out a Think Sheet (see page 146).

- When the time is up, the teacher should send the student back to your classroom.

This corrective action is highly effective with students who seek attention because they are removed from the peers whose attention they seek.

Major Infractions

No matter what system you use for delivering consequences, you must have a plan in place for dealing with severe misbehavior.

Sometimes you have to act quickly and decisively to stop a student's disruptive behavior. In cases of severe misbehavior, such as fighting, vandalism, defying a teacher or in some way stopping the entire class from functioning, a student must be removed immediately from the classroom.

Talk to your administrator about how major infractions will be dealt with and what support you can expect. Many schools have "Discipline Squads" consisting of two or three staff members who can be sent to a classroom to help remove a highly disruptive student.

How to Most Effectively Provide Consequences

Just as it is important to provide positive recognition in a manner that will be most effectively received by the difficult student, it is also important to individualize the manner in which you give consequences.

Here are some guidelines to follow when using consequences with a difficult student.

 ### Providing Consequences to Students Who Need Attention

Your number-one goal when providing consequences for these students is to give them the *minimal* amount of attention you possibly can. Remember, the whole reason they may have been disruptive in the first place was to gain attention. Don't *reward* their inappropriate behavior. They will take any kind of attention, good or bad. With these students, be as brief as possible. You may want to just write the student's name on your clipboard and simply say, "Doug, the direction was to work without talking. That's a warning."

That's all you need to say. If the disruptive behavior continues, keep your responses brief and to the point. "Doug, that's a check—one minute after class." Don't perseverate on the issue. Continue with your lesson. The student needs to learn that he or she will not get attention for misbehavior.

Providing Consequences to Students Who Need Firmer Limits

If you're confrontational (*"I've had it with you today. That's detention for you."*) or very public (*"OK, Jack has just earned himself detention again."*) when giving a consequence to this student, you're only going to get more confrontation in return and open the door to even more disruption.

With these students, stay calm, very calm. Don't raise your voice, and don't get upset. Speak quietly and avoid embarrassing the student. Walk over to the student and give him or her a choice to either comply with directions or choose to receive a corrective action.

For example:

> An eleventh-grade history teacher has given a direction to get started on an assignment. One student, Kristin, has paid no attention to the direction and begins to leaf through a magazine. The teacher walks over to Kristin's desk, leans down and speaks calmly to her.

> Teacher: (*in a soft voice*) Kristin, the directions are to take your notebook and a pencil out. You have a choice. You can follow these directions or you can wait one minute after class. The choice is yours, Kristin.

Also, give the student time to respond—time to save face.

Give them fifteen seconds. Believe it or not, most teachers don't even allow students five seconds to respond. They're so anxious to stop the unwanted behavior that they want the student to obey immediately.

You've got to give limit-seeking students time to save face. Let them huff. Let them puff. Let them go into slow motion. They need to do it. If they comply within fifteen seconds, you've achieved your goal. The student has chosen appropriate behavior.

Fifteen seconds, however, is long enough to wait. If a student doesn't comply within that amount of time then he or she probably isn't going to.

Providing Consequences to Students Who Need Motivation

Students who need motivation may need something different from you when it comes to consequences. Providing corrective actions such as time out and sending the student to another classroom won't motivate the student to begin or complete assignments, which is the student's primary problem. Unless the student is overtly disruptive or refuses to do work, the only action that must be taken with these students is that they are required to finish the assigned amount of work they are given. The student must recognize that you are not going away. If they do not finish the work in class, they will need to finish it at another time, whether at recess, lunch, after school, or at home.

For example:

- You will finish incomplete assignments at recess, lunch or before school.

- You will finish incomplete assignments during before-school detention or during after-school detention.

A seventh-grade class is working on an assignment. Gary, a student who needs motivation, is sitting at his desk staring at the paper with pencil in hand, but making no attempt to do the work. His teacher walks over to him.

Teacher: Gary, I expect you to do this assignment today. You have a choice. You can finish it now, in class, or you can come back to the room after you eat and finish it then. It's up to you, Gary."

You must hold difficult students accountable, and you must have tools to do so. On the other hand, the last thing you want to do is *rely* on consequences to manage behavior. Consequences are not an end in and of themselves, but a part of the relationship-building process. They are designed to teach, not punish. If you use consequences to "get" kids, you won't get anywhere. Most difficult students have had enough neglect, abuse, anger and disapproval. What they have not had enough of is a positive relationship with their teacher.

In using consequences with difficult students, remember that this is not the only behavior management effort you are making with this student. Day in and day out you're always working on establishing a positive relationship built on trust and high expectations. Any corrective actions you take must go hand in hand with your ongoing objective of establishing this positive relationship.

Consequences alone will not teach students to choose responsible behavior. Combined with clearly communicated expectations and consistent positive support, however, they can guide a difficult student toward choosing the appropriate behavior he or she needs to be successful in school.

Summary

Meeting the special needs of difficult students starts by recognizing that these students are not like your other students. Difficult students are driven by real unmet needs that prompt them to choose inappropriate, destructive and noncompliant behavior.

If you are going to have any success with a difficult student, you must first identify the need that motivates his or her behavior. From there, you can individualize your efforts in a manner that meets that need, and thus frees the student to move forward.

Throughout every effort you make with this student, the positive relationship must continue to be enhanced. Every success is an opportunity to build even more success. And every setback is an opportunity to communicate your trust and expectations that the student can succeed, and can make better choices the next time.

The tenacity and commitment you demonstrate will be the factor that moves the student toward the Trust Line.

COMMUNICATING WITH DIFFICULT STUDENTS

Communicating with Difficult Students

Difficult students will argue, be confrontational, critical, angry, verbally abusive, sullen, insulting and rude. When you're on the receiving end, it's all too easy to react emotionally and respond with anger or irritation.

These responses will not build trust or enhance your relationship with the student, nor will they help the student to comply.

Communicating with a difficult student requires planning and specific skills. You need to know how to avoid reactive responses, and how to focus your energies on helping the student make better behavioral choices.

The communication skills presented in this section of *Succeeding With Difficult Students* will help you break through the barriers that stand in the way of effective communication. They will also ensure that all of your interactions with students are directed toward building trusting, positive relationships.

Defusing Confrontations

Teacher: Class, please take out your notebooks and begin writing the answers to the questions that are on the board. This is an open book quiz so you may use your textbook.

The teacher scans the room as students begin to get out their materials and start to work. After a few moments she sees that Jason, a difficult student in her class, hasn't made a move to get started.

Teacher: Jason, it's time to get to work.

Jason sullenly looks up at her.

Jason: I don't feel like it today. Just stay off my case, okay?

Angered by the hostile response, the teacher reacts instantly to Jason's words.

Teacher: I didn't ask you if you feel like it or not, Jason. Take your notebook out and get started.

Jason: (*with increased hostility*) Back off. I told you I don't want to.

Teacher: (*angrier*) I heard what you said. Now you hear what I say. Get your notebook out and start writing. Everyone else seems to be able to get to work. I think you can, too.

Jason: (*mumbling under his breath*) You want it done so
           bad, then do it yourself.

Teacher: What did you say?

Jason: I didn't say anything. (*He looks around the class
           for support*). Nobody said anything, right?
           Maybe you're hearing things.

Other kids laugh along with him. And as other students
become involved, the teacher's anxiety increases.

Teacher: That's it, Jason. I've had enough of this. Keep this
           up and you won't be out of detention till the end
           of the year.

Jason: Yeah? Well the end of the year is now. I'm out
           of here.

Jason gets up and storms out of the classroom.

What happened?

In less than thirty seconds a simple direction to begin work has escalated
into a no-win confrontation that will carry negative repercussions for
everyone involved.

- Jason maneuvered himself (with a little help from the teacher) into a
  corner where the only possible way he could save face was to escalate
  the situation until it was out of control.

- The teacher reacted emotionally and in anger to Jason's initial
  comments. Her subsequent responses fed into Jason's need to control.
  She was part of the reason the behavior escalated. Now she's got an
  even more difficult situation to deal with. Jason has walked
  out of class.

- The teacher's relationship with Jason has worsened.

- The entire class is off task and instructional time has been lost.

> One of the toughest situations a teacher faces in dealing
> with difficult students is when a student confronts his or her
> authority in a highly emotional manner. These are the
> situations teachers dread. These are the situations that
> cause a lot of stress and anxiety.

Unfortunately, these situations are also inevitable. When you set limits and hold difficult students accountable—as you must—*there will be confrontations.*

When most students are given a direction to do something, or even when given a consequence, their reaction may be a groan, a mumbled complaint or, at most, a glare across the room. With difficult students, however, the response is often far more emotional and manipulative. These students are accustomed to intimidating teachers. They know the emotional buttons to push. They know how to get the responses that will meet their needs. The student who needs firmer limits knows just how to take control in a confrontation. The student who needs attention knows how to get plenty of that, too.

Remember too that these students do not automatically trust that anything you say or request is in their best interest. They will resist, and they will often fight you every inch of the way.

A difficult student, therefore, can often be confrontational. If you are going to help the student through the confrontation, and help yourself avoid unnecessary stress and anxiety, you need to be prepared to deal with these situations in a calm, proactive manner.

As always, preparation and planning are the key.

As we have mentioned before, human beings respond physiologically to conflict. We can't help it. Faced with highly emotional situations, the heart beats faster, neck muscles tighten, the stomach turns and adrenaline surges. As a result, we are triggered into immediately reacting to the situation at hand, not into calmly assessing it. And when we react it's all too easy to become angry, make inappropriate comments, and ultimately escalate the confrontation. That's what you saw taking place in the opening scenario.

Proactive teachers plan their responses to volatile situations. They know the steps they need to take to stay calm and they know what to do to stay in control of the situation and of their own emotions.

How you stay in control and defuse a confrontation depends upon how you respond to that student. You are the key. It's in your hands whether this situation will become a war or dissipates into a difficult situation that can be handled.

In order to keep control of the situation, you'll have to first keep control of your natural responses. To do that, you must remain calm.

How to Stay Calm When a Student Confronts You

When a student becomes confrontational, your first and most natural reaction is to become angry and to speak even more forcefully to get the student to do what you want.

Here's a sequence of techniques to use that will help counteract your body's natural inclination to react emotionally:

1. Do not speak. Remain calm.

Tell yourself, "Stay calm." Do not speak to the student right away. Instead, direct your attention first toward calming yourself and giving yourself the opportunity to take control of the situation.

2. Use deep breathing techniques.

Take a slow, deep breath. This will help relax you and ease the tension that is quickly building up. It will help to counteract the anxiety that is rising, and the need you may be feeling to react with anger or irritation to the student.

3. Count to three, four or five.

By counting to yourself, and combining it with deep breathing, you will not only be silent but you will begin to relax.

4. Depersonalize the situation.

Don't take what's going on personally when a student gets upset. Intellectualize the experience. Remind yourself that the student is not mounting a personal attack aimed just at you. Rather the student is responding in a manner that is consistent with his past experiences, his lack of trust and his own needs.

It's not personal.

Some teachers even find it helpful to view the situation for the moment as a television program or movie, reminding themselves that *this isn't about me!* By depersonalizing the situation, you make it easier to control your own emotions.

> Remember, the calmer you remain during a confrontation, the more control you will have over the situation as it unfolds.

And the calmer you remain, the harder it will be for the student to remain upset. Always keep in mind that it takes two people to have an argument.

Now, what do you do after you've calmed yourself?

You have to, of course, deal with the student's behavior.

Let's look first at the types of confrontations you encounter.

Covert vs. Overt Confrontations

Confrontations with students take two different forms: covert and overt.

A **covert confrontation** occurs when a student responds to you with a sneer, a dirty look, mumbles under his or her breath or does something hostile that others in the class are unaware of.

An **overt confrontation** is when a student just blatantly comes after you and the whole class is aware of it. The student may verbally defy your authority, be insulting, or talk back. There is no mistaking an overt confrontation.

It's important to identify the type of confrontation you are dealing with because you need to handle each in a different manner.

Let's look first at covert confrontations.

Covert Confrontations

A fifth-grader, Amanda, has stopped doing her assignment and instead is doodling on her paper and aimlessly humming to herself. Noticing that she is off task, the teacher tells Amanda to get back to work. Amanda responds by rolling her eyes, making a face and mimicking the teacher's request under her breath. (*"All right, Amanda, get back to work."*)

What does the teacher do now?

Here's what often happens:

> The teacher feels both hurt and angered by Amanda's response. These feelings compel him to quickly react to Amanda's behavior—to call her on it and put a stop to it.
>
> Teacher: Amanda, what did you say?
>
> Amanda: (*giggling under her breath*) Nothing, Mr. Johnson. I didn't say anything.
>
> Teacher: (*irritation and anger creeping into his voice*) Amanda, I want you to stop making faces and stop giggling and get to work.
>
> Amanda: (*defensively*) I'm not making any faces.
>
> Teacher: (*with increasing anger*) Amanda, if you think I'm going to allow you to make rude remarks and rude faces in this classroom you're wrong.
>
> Amanda: (*angrily shouting back*) I told you I didn't say anything. Why are you always picking on me? Nobody heard me say anything. What's your problem?
>
> Teacher: Fine, Amanda. If that's the way you feel, I guess you won't mind going to time out.
>
> Amanda: (*yelling*) What am I getting punished for? I told you I didn't say anything. You're never fair. You're always out to get me.

Result? An incident that started out very small ended up larger than life and very confrontational. And, most important, nothing positive was accomplished in the end.

Amanda did not get on task, and the relationship between Amanda and her teacher has taken a turn for the worse.

The situation did not have to end this way. The way in which you respond to a covert confrontation can mean the difference between defusing the confrontation and moving on, or escalating the confrontation and having a worse problem on your hands.

Here's what to do when presented with a covert confrontation.

First, calm yourself.

Use the previously mentioned calming techniques to decrease your anxiety and your body's natural inclination to react. Stay calm. Count to three, four or five. Take a deep breath.

Say to yourself, "Do not get angry. Don't get upset." Remind yourself not to take it personally. It's not about you.

Next, disengage from the student.

What do you feel like doing when a student sneers at you, gives you a dirty look or mumbles something rude under his or her breath (but just loud enough so that you can hear it)?

You react in a very human manner. You feel angry! And the first thing you may be compelled to do is make comments like "Don't give me that look, young lady," or "What did you just say?"

These responses are an invitation to the student to argue.

You're literally asking the student to respond and get involved confrontationally. After all, how is the student likely to respond? Because it was covert, the student will of course deny the allegation.

> "I didn't make a face at you."

> "I didn't say anything."

Suddenly you've boxed yourself into a "yes you did" corner that is unresolvable. And the reality is that you are getting caught up in secondary behaviors rather than focusing on whether the student is complying with your request to get on task.

Get some distance. Step away from the student. By putting distance between the two of you, you will give the student an opening to save face, back down and choose the appropriate behavior you need. You will also give yourself some additional calming moments, too.

> Remember, if the confrontation escalates, the student will be far less likely to choose appropriate behavior. Keep your real goal in mind.

If necessary, speak to the student later.

If you were to address the student's behavior right now, in front of the class, where would it go? Straight toward escalation. The student would suddenly have an audience and you would be dealing with a far more difficult situation. Of course you cannot necessarily allow covert, confrontational behavior to go ignored. You have a responsibility to hold a student accountable for his or her behavior. You can, however, deal with it later. Let the student know that you will speak with him or her about it, but later, after class or after school. If necessary, you can provide the student a consequence at that time for inappropriate behavior. The consequence can then be given without other students around who may serve as an audience and fuel the confrontation.

Now let's see how a teacher more effectively handles Amanda's covert confrontational behavior.

Scene: When Amanda's teacher tells her to get to work, Amanda sneers at the teacher and mumbles under her breath. Amanda's covert response is not lost on her teacher, but instead of becoming angry, he takes a calming deep breath, counts to five and purposely moves away from Amanda's desk. As irritating as the behavior is, he lets it pass for the moment and focuses instead on whether or not Amanda gets to work.

He gives Amanda a little time and space to make a choice.

Keep in mind that his responses to Amanda are not coming out of a vacuum. This teacher has been building trust and establishing a positive relationship with Amanda all year long. He has already taken many steps to demonstrate to Amanda that he cares about her and that he is confident that Amanda will succeed in his class. He's now demonstrating that confidence. The teacher is communicating his high expectations by giving Amanda the opportunity, in a nonconfrontational manner, to make a good choice. He's showing Amanda that he trusts her.

In this case, his strategy paid off. Amanda chose to get back on task. And at the same time Amanda made this responsible choice, she also moved up one more notch toward the Trust Line, feeling more assured that this teacher is, in fact, on her side.

Later, as Amanda is working, the teacher walks by her desk and gives her a quick thumbs up.

Now let's see what can happen when a teacher is involved in an overt confrontation.

Overt Confrontations

An eighth-grade teacher is monitoring her students as they take an English test. One student, Terry, keeps rustling his paper, tapping his pencil and bothering other students around him. The teacher notices his off-task behavior and speaks to him.

Teacher: Terry, I want you to settle down now and get to work on that test.

Terry slams his pencil down and angrily brushes his test paper off his desk and onto the floor.

Terry: (*with hostility*) I don't feel like taking any test today.

What happens next?

Here's what often happens when a teacher is confronted by such overt defiance:

The teacher reacts immediately to Terry's hostile challenge. Her anxiety and her anger rise quickly. She feels a need to put a quick end to the challenge.

Teacher: Terry, pick up that paper and get to work. Now.

Terry: You pick it up. I said I'm not taking any test.

Teacher: (*walking over to Terry's desk*) Pick up that paper, Terry. You don't decide what you will and what you won't do in this class. Do you understand me?

All attention in the classroom turns to Terry and the teacher. Test taking is halted for the moment.

Terry: (*voice rising, aware that everyone is looking at him*) I understand I'm not picking up that pencil and I understand that I'm not taking the test.

Teacher: (*pointing to the paper on the floor and speaking angrily and loudly*) Terry, I've had enough of your attitude and your mouth. Now are you going to pick up that paper or do you want me to call Mr. Simons?

Terry: Do what you want. You're the one who decides what to do in this class, remember?

In an overt confrontation a student very openly and very defiantly challenges the teacher. Overt confrontations are more difficult to deal with than covert ones because they are often volatile, threatening and grab the attention of the entire class.

It is in situations like these that a teacher's anxiety can escalate most rapidly. Unfortunately, the first reaction is usually to fight back. If you are to deal successfully with overt confrontations you have to have something more effective to turn to than your hurt feelings or anger.

> Overt confrontations require careful, skilled responses.

Here's what to do:

First, use calming techniques.

You may be taken by surprise or caught off guard, but don't let one word escape from your mouth before you take the opportunity to calm yourself. Take a deep breath and count. Tell yourself, "This student is very angry. He wants me to argue with him. I am not going to argue. I am going to stay calm. It's not personal."

Next, use a paradoxical response.

What does a difficult student expect when he or she is defiant, talks back and refuses to comply with a request? The student expects what he or she usually receives: anger, ultimatums and more confrontation.

Take a different approach. To defuse the immediate situation, respond in the exact opposite way the student expects you to. If the student is shouting, speak softly. If the student yells even louder, speak more softly still. This technique will put the student off guard and help you deescalate the immediate situation.

> Remember the paradox: The calmer you get, the more difficult it will be for the student to escalate the situation.

By responding paradoxically, you demonstrate that you're in control and are staying in control. You are not becoming part of an argument.

When you do respond, what do you say to the student?

The key to an effective paradoxical response is to use what is called a refocusing technique.

First, put yourself inside the student's emotional turmoil and acknowledge his or her feelings. They are, after all, real to the student. Then, calmly refocus the conversation back to what you need him or her to do.

Let's look again at the exchange between Terry and his teacher. This time we will see the teacher respond in a proactive, more effective manner, using a paradoxical response and refocusing techniques:

> Teacher: Terry, I want you to settle down now and get to
> work on that test.

> Terry slams his pencil down and angrily brushes his paper
> off his desk and onto the floor.

Terry: (*angrily*) I don't feel like taking any test today.

The teacher says nothing right away. Instead, she takes a deep calming breath, counts to five and reminds herself that Terry's anger has nothing to do with her. When she addresses Terry, she is in control. She ignores the paper on the floor and instead speaks very quietly and very calmly.

Teacher: (*calmly, in a low voice*) I can see that you don't want to take the test, Terry. I hear that you really don't want to, but it's your responsibility and you need to do it.

She acknowledges the student's feelings, then refocuses her comments on what she wants the student to do.

Terry: I don't care. I don't want to take it.

Teacher: (*even more calmly and quietly*) It's clear to me that you really don't want to take this test today, Terry. I hear you. I do. But it's your job to take the test.

The teacher continues to acknowledge what the student is feeling in a calm, nonconfrontational manner, then restates what she needs the student to do.

By acknowledging Terry's feelings, the teacher gives him respect and acknowledges that those feelings, however inappropriate, are real. Even in a difficult situation like this the positive relationship is enhanced, rather than torn down.

Of course, there still is no guarantee that the student will comply. If he or she continues to defy you, you will need to take further action:

If necessary, move the student away from peers.

If refocusing or a paradoxical response does not work, and the student continues to be confrontational, you may need to have the student move away from the rest of the class so you can speak to him or her privately. By removing the student from his or her audience, you lessen the likelihood of the student feeling compelled to act even tougher.

If, for example, Terry continues to refuse to begin his test, the teacher asks him to walk over to the side of the classroom with her.

> *Away from the rest of the class, the teacher speaks to Terry:*

Teacher: *(very calmly)* Terry, I want you to succeed in my class. You've done some excellent work this semester, and you deserve to have that grade you've worked so hard for. But Terry, by not taking this test you're making a choice that's going to hurt you. I can see that maybe something is going on that's upsetting you today, and we can talk about that later. Right now, I'm really concerned that you make a choice that's good for you.

This brief discussion, away from the class, gives the teacher the opportunity to quietly let Terry know she cares about the choices he's making for himself. It also gives Terry another chance to make a better choice. Because this conversation is taking place out of the earshot of other students he can choose to comply without losing face. He may return to his desk with a lot of attitude and under-the-breath remarks, but the teacher ignores the covert behavior. He's making a good choice and that is the behavior to focus on.

Tough Situations

What if the student refuses to leave the peer group?

If the student should simply refuse to leave the peer group and/or continues to confront you, you need to have back-up. If appropriate, an administrator support team should be contacted and the student physically removed from the room. In the meantime, if you are concerned about a physical confrontation, move yourself away from the student but do not turn your back on him or her.

If there is no physical back-up available, you may simply have to tell the student, "I can't make you do that now." Let the student stay in his or her seat and deal with the situation later.

Sometimes you have to choose to back off.

Here are two other situations in which backing off is the recommended course of action to take:

• Back off if the student's behavior is out of character.

If a student's overtly confrontational behavior is an erratic departure from the norm, there may be something wrong that is affecting him or her. If this is the case, it is much more appropriate to let the matter go for the moment and discuss it later, away from the class, when some time has passed. Give the student some space to work out whatever it is that's upsetting him or her. Be sure to follow up later with a talk.

> Caroline is a ninth-grade student who generally gets along well with her peers and teachers. Her English teacher has just asked the class to take out their notebooks. Instead of complying as she usually does, Caroline slams all of her books onto the floor, crosses her arms across her chest, glares at the teacher and says, "Forget it."
>
> This behavior is so out of character for Caroline that the teacher chooses to ignore it for the moment. Ten minutes later, when the rest of the class is working independently,

he goes over to Caroline, leans down and speaks calmly to her: "Caroline, is there something upsetting you? Would you like to talk to me about it?"

• Back off if the student is extremely violent or volatile.

If you feel that a student is about to become violent or completely lose control it's best to back off. Intervention at this point would only disrupt the class further, put you and students at risk, and possibly escalate the situation beyond controllable means.

You must, however, address the behavior at a later time. Don't ignore it. Part of building trust is letting the student know that you won't back down on your expectations. If you cannot safely deal with a specific situation at the moment, the student must understand that it will be dealt with.

Confrontations with difficult students are inevitable. However, as the student continues to build trust in you and a positive relationship develops, these confrontations will become less frequent and less difficult. But don't expect changes to happen overnight. For some students, change may come very slowly. For others change may not come at all while you are the student's teacher.

> Keep the big picture in mind. Do not let confrontations shake your resolve to make a difference with this student.

Confrontations are hurtful, anger provoking and frustrating. But they are part of dealing with difficult students. Do not look at a confrontation as a setback. Instead view it as another opportunity to drive home to the student the fact that you are committed to helping him or her. The calm, firm but caring way that you handle a confrontation will go a long way toward building trust with the student.

One-to-One Problem Solving

"The greatest impact I have with a difficult student is when we sit down, just the two of us, to try to work out solutions to tough problems. These kids often need the kind of one-to-one attention that only happens when we do that. It is through these conferences that I can really help a student assume more responsibility for his or her behavior. I almost always leave these meetings feeling that the relationship is stronger and more positive, and the student is better positioned to make more responsible choices."

When a difficult student continues to have behavior problems, providing a consequence may stop the misbehavior for the moment, but by itself it will not help the student learn to make better choices in the future.

When misbehavior continues, this student needs to receive more in-depth and personal guidance from you. It's time to sit down in a one-to-one problem-solving conference, listen to the student's concerns, firmly clarify your own expectations, and then work together to arrive at a practical course of action.

The goal of this meeting is not to punish, but to provide caring and guidance to a student who needs plenty of both. It's a chance to listen, to find out what the student is feeling and thinking, and a chance to build your relationship. The overall tone of the meeting should be a message of both commitment *and* of firmness:

> "I care about you. I am committed to doing everything I can to help you be successful. I want you to be successful, but I will not allow you to disrupt the classroom."

When should you consider meeting with a student in a one-to-one problem-solving conference?

Listen to your own instincts. If you are concerned about a student's behavior and feel he or she will benefit from such a meeting, by all means do it.

Here are some guidelines:

- **Meet with a student in a one-to-one problem-solving conference when inappropriate behavior is chronic.**

  If misbehavior continues in spite of all the efforts you have made, it is time to work with the student to both clarify your expectations and structure some alternative actions the student can take.

- **Meet with a student in a one-to-one problem-solving conference when there is a sudden behavior change.**

  If a student suddenly behaves in an uncharacteristic, disruptive manner, you need to find out why. A one-to-one problem-solving conference will give you the opportunity to hear the student out and to demonstrate that you care and are there to help.

- **Meet with a student in a one-to-one problem-solving conference when there is a serious problem.**

  Serious problems such as fighting cannot be overlooked. In addition to whatever consequence the student has received, you need to help them redirect their anger.

Often when a teacher meets with a student under any of these circumstances the meeting becomes a lecture from teacher to student, with the teacher overreacting to the student's behavior problems, doing all the talking and setting a punitive tone to the meeting.

For example:

> A teacher and student are meeting after class to talk about the student's chronic behavior problems.

Teacher: Gerry, can you give me one good reason why I should put up with your constant disruptions in class?

Gerry: I don't know.

Teacher: I know you don't know. But I know I'm not going to put up with this any longer. You've gotten away with disturbing the class long enough and I'm through with it. You're not the only student in this class. Do you understand me?

This approach will turn off communication, and that is not what a one-to-one problem-solving conference is about. A one-to-one problem-solving conference is about arriving at solutions together.

For many difficult students, this meeting may be the only time an adult has ever taken the time and interest to sit down and talk to them in a caring manner about their behavior. Consequently, the importance of the meeting is immense. Let the student know you are truly there for him or her.

The purpose of a one-to-one problem-solving conference therefore is twofold:

One, it's an opportunity to further build your relationship with the student.

Two, it's an opportunity to assure the student that you are committed to his or her success—that you have expectations for this student and you are going to do everything you can to see that these expectations are met.

Conducting a One-to-One Problem-Solving Conference

Follow these guidelines when conducting a problem-solving conference with a difficult student:

Meet privately with the student.

This conference needs to be confidential. Be sure there are no other students around to overhear or disrupt your meeting. The meeting should also be brief, a maximum of 10 to 15 minutes. Keep in mind that this is not a consulting session; your goal is not to do therapy. Rather, the goal of a one-to-one problem-solving conference is to help the student explore alternative, more appropriate behaviors.

Show empathy and concern.

Remember that this meeting is not about you and it's not about your classroom.

A one-to-one problem-solving conference is about your student. It's about taking an extra step in helping the student so that he or she can choose more appropriate behavior.

Your conference, therefore, must focus on helping the student gain insight into his or her present behavior and understand why he or she needs to choose more responsible behavior. Through your words and attitude, let the student know you are concerned and that you care. Be sure the student knows you are having the meeting because you care and want to help, not because you want to embarrass or punish.

Let your opening words set the tone of the meeting and communicate that concern:

> "Evan, I can see you had a hard time controlling your anger in class today. I'm concerned about that because I know that it can be difficult getting along with students sitting near you. I also know that you don't like it when I send you to time out. Let's take some time to talk about this."

> "Kerry, I can see that it's hard for you to keep your mind on work when you are with your group. I'm concerned about this because you're not getting your work done and that's not good for you. I want you to do the very best you can in this class. Let's talk a bit now about what we can do together to solve this problem."

Question the student to find out why there is a problem.

Don't assume you know why a student is misbehaving or having a problem. Listen to the student's point of view. Question him or her to find out what the problem may be. Is there something happening at home, with other students or with a particular student that is upsetting? Is the work too hard?

The student may resist, and you may not learn anything, but give your student a chance to express himself. Show you respect the student as an individual with valid concerns that you are interested in listening to.

You have a responsibility to treat your students with respect. Do not, therefore, ask questions that communicate negative expectations and close off effective communication:

"What is your problem, David?"

"Jackie, do you think you're going to get away with this any longer?"

"Can you give me one good reason, Leslie, why I should put up with this?"

Question the student in a manner that shows caring, concern and a real interest in helping. Here are some questions that will open the door to communication.

"David, can you tell me what's causing you to be upset?"

"Jackie, is there a reason you're having such a bad day?"

"Is there something going on that you want to tell me about, Leslie?"

Asking the question is just the beginning. After you ask a question, *listen* to the student. Don't interrupt. Let the student talk. This may be one of very few times the student has been listened to by an adult.

Determine what you can do to help.

After listening to what the student has to say, you may discover there is a simple answer that will get him or her back on track. For example, if a student is having trouble with other students in class, all you may need to do is move his or her seat. If a student who sits in the back of the room is having trouble staying on task, it may help to move him or her forward.

It's unlikely that the problem will be solved so easily, but it's always worth considering.

Determine how the student can improve his or her behavior.

Focus part of your meeting on what the student can choose to do differently in the future that will enable him or her to handle the problem more effectively. Talk about the situation. Listen to the student's input. If need be, teach new behaviors to the student (see pages 86-89 for an age-specific review of teaching appropriate behavior).

> "I hear that you're having trouble with the other boys, but fighting is not allowed in this classroom. Let's talk about other ways you can deal with these situations. What do you think you can do rather than fight?"

> "I hear that it's hard for you to keep your mind on your work when you're with your group. Let's talk about things you can do that might help you do your work better."

State your own expectations about how the student is to behave.

Make no mistake, in spite of the empathetic and caring attitude you are communicating, the student must clearly understand that you are very serious about not allowing misbehavior to continue. He or she must understand that under no circumstances will you allow the student to engage in disruptive behavior.

> "I'm going to work with you to solve this problem. You're a good student and you're smart. I know you can behave responsibly. But remember, fighting is not acceptable in class. Anytime you choose to fight, you will be choosing to go to the principal."

If necessary, disarm the student's criticism.

Don't be surprised if a difficult student, particularly a student who is confrontational, blames you for his or her problems. A difficult student may be openly critical of you and critical of the way you handle just about everything.

> "You're always picking on me."
>
> "If you gave me work I could do I wouldn't have to ask everyone for help all the time."
>
> "It's all Theo's fault but you never get him in trouble."
>
> "You never notice me when I'm good. You only notice when you think I'm doing something wrong."

What usually happens when someone criticizes us? We become defensive and often try to justify ourselves.

> "Sara, I do not always pick on you."
>
> "Tom, I don't give you work you can't do."
>
> "Of course Theo gets in trouble when he does something wrong."
>
> "Debbie, I do too pay attention when you're good."

Defensiveness is a natural reaction to accusations, but reactive, defensive responses will not help build your relationship with the student and will undermine your role as a leader. Instead of reacting, allow the student to have his or her say—then step in and disarm the criticism.

Here's what to do:

First, listen to what the student has to say.

Student: You're always picking on me. You're always on my case. You never get after anyone else.

Validate the student's feelings. Show that you do understand that the student is upset.

Then ask the student to be specific in his or her criticism.

Teacher: (*calmly*) I see how upset you are. Can you give me some examples of how I pick on you?

Student: You know, like all the time. All the time you're after me and none of the other kids.

Teacher: Can you tell me how I pick on you, Donna? Can you give me an example of what you mean so I can better understand why you're so upset?

Disarming criticism has the same effect on a student as a paradoxical response. It is a response that is opposite from what the student expects. By disarming a student's criticism of you, you can calm the student down. Instead of an expected fight, the student is faced with a concerned, empathetic adult. When you disarm criticism you open up communication so you can more effectively continue your talk.

Your interest and caring will build the student's trust and respect.

Focus on the student's needs during a one-to-one conference.

As with all interactions with a difficult student, keep in mind the primary need that he or she is trying to fulfill. Let that information guide you in shaping your responses.

Students who need attention.

For these students, the simple fact that you are meeting together will fulfil his or her needs for the moment. You have to be firm and make sure that you impress upon the student that this meeting has a serious purpose— that there's a problem to be solved and that you intend to work with the student to solve it.

Students who need firm limits.

You will have to be prepared for the fact that these students will be very critical of you. They'll blame you for their problems. They'll say it's your fault. So be prepared and don't react to it when it happens. Don't get defensive. Disarm the student's criticism and stay firm.

Students who need motivation.

During a one-to-one conference with these students you're going to have to be very direct. You've got to get them motivated to do their work. Your expectations must be firmly and clearly stated. "In this classroom I expect you to do your work."

Document the meeting.

Whenever you have a one-to-one meeting with a student, be sure to document what is said. This information may be valuable for you to share with either the student's parents and/or your administrator and/or support staff.

Sample One-to-One Problem-Solving Conference

This sample conference shows how a teacher integrates all the elements we've talked about into an effective meeting with a difficult student.

Michael is a sixth-grade student who has had a lot of trouble staying out of arguments and fights. In spite of all the teacher's efforts to help Michael make better behavior choices, these fights in the classroom have recently increased in frequency.

He and the teacher are meeting after school to discuss the situation and work out some solutions.

The teacher opens the meeting by showing empathy and concern.

Start with statement of concern.

Teacher: Michael, I can see that you had a very difficult time in class today. You shoved Marco and you pushed several other students. You also called these students names. I'm really concerned about this, Michael, because I want you to succeed in my class and this behavior is hurting you. I know you don't like it when you are sent to time out. That's why I wanted to have this meeting with you. I want us both to figure out what we can do together to help you make better choices about how you handle things.

Now the teacher questions the student to find out why there is a problem.

Teacher: (*in a caring tone*) Is there something going on that you'd like to tell me about?

Michael: I don't know. Nothing, I guess.

Teacher: Michael, I care about you, and I'm listening. That's what we're both here for. If there's a problem, I'd like to hear it because I want to help if I can.

Michael: (*suddenly very upset*) It's not my fault! Marco and those guys make fun of me. You don't see them do it but they do. They always say stuff and then I get mad. Then you always get *me* in trouble. You always punish me even when it's not my fault. You don't care that it's always Marco or Steven.

The teacher takes steps to disarm Michael's criticism.

Teacher: (*very calmly*) I see how upset you are, Michael. Can you give me an example of how I get you in trouble when it's not your fault?

Michael: (*angrier*) You just always do. And then everyone laughs because I'm in trouble again.

Teacher: (*even more calmly*) Michael, can you tell me how I get you in trouble when it's not your fault? I want to understand why you're so upset.

Michael: (*calming down*) I told you. Kids are always bothering me and I get mad. Then you get *me* in trouble.

Teacher: Okay, Michael, I hear that some of the other kids are bothering you. I really do hear you. I can understand how that upsets you and makes you angry. But Michael, we're talking about you now, and I cannot allow you to push other students or call them names. That behavior isn't good for you or anyone else. And you're right. When I see you pushing or calling names I do have to do something about it. I can't allow you to do that in my classroom.

The teacher now focuses on what the student can do differently in the future.

Teacher: Michael, I think we can come up with some better solutions for you than fighting. Let's talk about other ways you can handle these situations. What do you think you can do rather than get angry?

Michael and his teacher then share ideas about alternative ways he can react to the students' teasing. She helps him see that his furious reaction is exactly what the other boys are after, and that when he is given a consequence they are only encouraged to do it again and again. With this awareness, Michael is able to look for alternative ways he can respond.

Now the teacher restates her expectations.

Teacher: Michael, I'm going to work with you to solve this problem. I think you've come up with some good ideas about how you can respond when these boys tease you.

But Michael, I need to emphasize one more time: disrupting in class is NOT okay. Anytime you choose to push or shove another student, or call a student names, you will be choosing to go to another classroom.

We've made a good start today. I'm sure that tomorrow will be a better day for you. Remember, I'm here to help you. We'll talk more and make sure the problem is getting solved.

A one-to-one problem-solving conference is a powerful tool that you can use anytime during the year when you feel a student will benefit from more personal attention and guidance. Few interventions offer a better opportunity to both build the positive relationship and develop practical answers to problems.

SECTION THREE
Summary

Difficult students are often masters at pushing the buttons that send teachers' tempers soaring. To avoid the reactive responses that are so detrimental to your relationship with a student, you need to develop skills that will allow you to stay in control of confrontational and challenging situations.

> When a student becomes increasingly upset or defiant you *can* stay calm and deescalate the situation.

> When meeting in a problem-solving conference with a student you *can* communicate both firmness and caring.

Effective communication skills will enable you to continue to build trust with a student even in difficult circumstances.

SECTION FOUR

ADDITIONAL STRATEGIES

Additional Strategies

By consistently applying the techniques and skills presented to this point in *Succeeding With Difficult Students*, you will be able to help the majority of your difficult students make better choices, improve their behavior and sustain that improvement for long periods of time.

There will, however, still be some students whose behavior does not improve to a level that is satisfactory to you, or who are not able to sustain the improvement beyond a very short period of time.

With these students, the behavior management strategies you have tried so far will need to be augmented with additional, even more individualized strategies.

Additional Strategies:
Individualized Behavior Plans

"Since the beginning of the school year, I've been working on developing a positive relationship with Sam. It hasn't been easy. But bit by bit he has responded to caring, consistency and the higher expectations I've had for him. I've used basic behavior management skills more effectively with Sam, too. I've taught and reinforced the behaviors he needs to work on, I've given him plenty of positive recognition when he chooses those behaviors and I've provided consequences when he doesn't. In addition, I've counseled with him one-to-one when I felt he needed guidance.

For Sam, though, this just hasn't been enough. He still disrupts the class. And when he does behave, it isn't for very long. I've got to do something more for him than what I've been doing."

How do you know when it is time to go beyond the behavior management efforts presented so far in this book? How can you tell when you need to turn to additional, stronger strategies in order to help a difficult student?

Follow these guidelines:

> If you have applied the techniques presented to this point and the student is still continually disruptive, off task, or is not completing assignments—you need to individualize further.

> If you have applied the techniques presented to this point and you find yourself giving more and more consequences, or the consequences that have been used are no longer effective—you need to individualize further.

> If you have applied the techniques presented to this point and you find yourself becoming more and more frustrated and angry with the student—you need to individualize further.

If any of these criteria apply to a difficult student in your class, you need to sit down and plan what more you can do to help the student be successful. This is *not* the time to give up. If you don't find a way to help this student, his or her behavior won't change, he or she will not achieve the expectations you hold, and your classroom will remain disrupted.

Develop an Individualized Behavior Plan for this student.

An Individualized Behavior Plan provides even more structured, more powerful interventions to help the student.

Such a plan includes the following:

- Specific behaviors required of the student
- More effective ways to motivate (positively reinforce) the student
- Stronger, more meaningful consequences for inappropriate behavior

> To be effective, an Individualized Behavior Plan must also
> be accompanied by specific relationship-building goals.

Developed with care, implemented fairly and consistently, and used as part of an ongoing, planned effort to build a positive relationship, an Individualized Behavior Plan can be an extremely effective tool for helping a difficult student learn to choose more appropriate behavior.

In this chapter we will look at three types of Individualized Behavior Plans:

Individualized Behavior Plan
Part One—Classroom Plans

A Classroom Plan allows you to provide a difficult student more structured intervention within your classroom. Teachers often turn first to this type of Individualized Behavior Plan when techniques as presented in this book have not proven effective.

The plan consists of the following:

1. **Specific behaviors** you expect of the student

2. **Positive support** you will give the student for choosing appropriate behavior

3. **Corrective action** you will take each time the student chooses inappropriate behavior

Follow these steps when developing an Individualized Classroom Plan for a difficult student:

Step 1: Select specific behaviors to focus on.
Use the student's behavior profile to select one or two (and only one or two) of the most disruptive or chronic behaviors exhibited by the student. Use the profile also to clarify the *appropriate* behavior you need from the student.

For example, the sample profile on the next page shows that this student talks out in class and does not keep his hands and feet to himself.

Behavior Profile: Phil

When Student Is Noncompliant	What Behaviors Take Place	Behaviors Needed
Independent seatwork	Talking out, pushing and shoving other students.	
Class discussion	Speaking without permission, bothering other students.	

These behaviors are preventing Phil from successfully doing his own work and are affecting the rest of the class. The behaviors the teacher will focus on with the Individualized Classroom Plan are, therefore:

- You will not talk without permission.
- You will keep hands, feet and objects to yourself.

Step 2: Develop a positive motivation system to help the student choose the appropriate behavior.

Once you have chosen the behavior(s) you want the student to focus on, you will need to plan how you will motivate the student to choose those behaviors.

You need to develop a positive motivation system especially for this student, and this student alone. This positive motivation system will consist of the following:

- A specified reward the student will earn for appropriate behavior

- The length of time you want the student to take to earn the reward

- How you will track and acknowledge appropriate behavior

Here are two examples of such a positive motivation system:

Elementary
- For each 30 minutes that you do not shout and you keep your hands and feet to yourself, you will receive a check on a tracking chart. When all of the spaces on the chart are checked off, you will earn a lunch with the teacher.

Middle School/Secondary
- For each period during which you do not talk back or refuse to work, you will receive a point. When you earn five points you will receive a certificate you can use at the cafeteria.

Here's how to design a positive motivation system:

First, choose a reward the student will earn.

Rewards and recognitions are important—they are graphic reminders to students that they *can* make responsible behavior choices. The positives you choose, therefore, must be meaningful enough to compel the student to change his or her behavior. Use the Student Interest Inventory and your own relationship with the student to help choose a reward that you know the student will care about.

For example:

 Students Who Need Attention

Students who need attention like to earn that attention:

- Lunch with the teacher
- Sit at teacher's desk during class for one week
- One-to-one meeting after school

 Students Who Need Limits

Students who need limits like to feel powerful and special. Therefore, they like to earn rewards such as:

- Special privileges
- The right to be a monitor
- The right to tutor
- The right to skip a homework assignment

Students Who Need Motivation

Because these students have such low motivation select the consequence with great care. Be sure it is one you can and will deliver consistently, and one that will meet the student's specific need.

> For example: material rewards, small toys, food, certificates for products from local merchants.

Next, decide how long you want the student to take to earn the reward.

Make sure the student is able to earn the reward quickly. It may be in one day or in one week, depending on the age of the student. The younger or more immature the student, the more quickly the reward needs to be earned. Use your professional judgement in determining how quickly the student needs to earn the recognition.

Finally, determine how frequently you will acknowledge the student's appropriate behavior en route to earning the reward.

Once you decide how quickly you want the student to earn the reward, you need to plan how you will reinforce and track his or her appropriate behavior. Most teachers use a point system, stickers, or stamps on a chart to provide ongoing recognition before the reward itself is earned. Whatever method you use, set goals for yourself—for example, the student will earn ten points or stickers per day.

A rule of thumb is to reinforce the student as frequently as he or she exhibited the inappropriate behavior.

For example, if the student talks out in class approximately every fifteen minutes, plan to reinforce the student every fifteen minutes when he or she is *not* talking out.

Remind yourself to reinforce!

Once you've set goals, put a note in your plan book or a sticker on your watch to remind yourself to be on the lookout for the student's appropriate behavior. His or her success depends on your consistency in recognizing the appropriate behavior.

Step 3: Select consequences.

Under the terms of an Individualized Behavior Plan, a consequence must be given every time the student engages in inappropriate behavior. No warnings. No hierarchy of lesser consequences. At this point, a student needs to know that inappropriate behavior means a definite consequence—every time.

Because of this, you need to select the consequence with great care. Be sure it is one you can and will deliver consistently, and one that will meet the student's specific need.

For example:

 Students Who Need Attention

Corrective actions that work best with students who need attention are those that isolate them from their peers and the attention they want.

- Time out in another classroom (see page 149)
- Lunch detention
- After-school detention

Students Who Need Limits

These students believe they can intimidate you and act as though they do not care about any limits you set. Because they are in a power struggle with you, you need to provide the firmest limits possible.

- Tape record the student's behavior (see page 148)

- Have student call parents (see pages 148-149)

- Time out in another classroom (see page 149)

 Students Who Need Motivation

Your goal with these students is for them to complete assigned work. For this reason, all consequences included in an Individualized Classroom Plan should be related to finishing the assignment.

- Incomplete work will be finished at after-school or lunch detention.

On the following pages are sample Individualized Classroom Behavior Plans for students who need attention, students who need limits and students who need motivation. Notice that the positive reinforcement and consequences have been chosen with the student's specific needs in mind.

Use these samples as a reference for putting together your own individualized plans.

Individualized Classroom Behavior Plan for a Student Who Needs Attention
Elementary

Behaviors

- You will not talk without permission.

- You will stay in your seat.

Positive Support

- For each 30 minutes that you do not talk out in class and you stay in your seat, you will receive a stamp on your chart.

- When your chart is filled, you will earn lunch with the teacher.

Corrective Action

If you continue to shout and get out of your seat and run around the classroom, you will be sent to another room for 30 minutes to calm down.

This behavior contract is highly individualized for this attention-seeking student. The positive recognition the student will earn has been chosen to meet his or her need for attention. Lunch with the teacher is a meaningful reward to a student who enjoys such attention from the teacher. Likewise, the consequence of being sent to another room, away from peers, for 30 minutes is a deterrent that will carry weight.

Individualized Classroom Behavior Plan for a Student Who Needs Attention
Middle/Secondary

Behaviors

- You will not make inappropriate comments, jokes or gestures.

Positive Support

- For every period you spend with no inappropriate behavior, you will receive a point.

- When you have received 5 points, you will earn the right to skip one homework assignment of your choice.

Corrective Action

- Every time you engage in inappropriate behavior, you will be given detention.

- The teacher will check to make sure you attended detention.

Individualized Classroom Behavior Plan for a Student Who Needs Limits
Elementary

Behaviors

- You will follow directions; you will not argue.

- You will not argue or fight with other students.

Positive Support

- Each hour you do not argue or refuse to work, you will receive a point.

- When you earn 10 points, you have the right to select the monitor job you want for the day.

Corrective Action

- You will be sent to another classroom for 30 minutes each time you are disruptive.

- If you refuse to go to another classroom, you will be escorted to the principal's office.

Individualized Classroom Behavior Plan for a Student Who Needs Limits
Middle/Secondary

Behaviors

- You will follow directions and not talk back.

- You will do assigned work.

Positive Support

- For each period during which you do not talk back or refuse to work, you will receive a point.

- When you earn five points, you will get a certificate for a free lunch at school.

Corrective Action

- Whenever you talk back or do not do assigned work the teacher will accompany you to the office to call your parents.

- You will explain to your parents why they are being called.

- If you refuse to go to the office, the Discipline Squad will help remove you from the classroom.

Individualized Classroom Behavior Plan for a Student Who Needs Motivation
Elementary

Behaviors

- You will complete assignments.

- You will participate in class activities.

Positive Support

- Each day, a student from an upper-level class will be available to tutor you for half an hour.

- For each assignment you complete, you will receive a point. When you have earned 10 points, you may choose a prize.

Corrective Action

- You will finish incomplete assignments at recess, lunch or before school.

Individualized Classroom Behavior Plan for a Student Who Needs Motivation
Middle/Secondary

Behaviors

- You will complete assignments.

- You will participate in class activities.

Positive Support

- Two times a week you will have a peer tutor for the period.

- For each class or homework assignment you complete, you will receive a point. When you have earned 10 points, you will receive a gift certificate from a local merchant.

Corrective Action

- You will finish incomplete assignments during before-school detention or during after-school detention.

Continue to Build the Positive Relationship

An Individualized Classroom Behavior Plan will provide additional structure for a difficult student, but the other half of the equation—a positive relationship—must also be present if the student is to succeed.

It is absolutely essential that you continue to take the time to work on your relationship with the student. As you develop the student's plan, set specific relationship-building goals for yourself. It is this extra attention that will continue to have the greatest impact with the student.

For example:

- Spend time problem solving with the student on a one-to-one basis.

- Attend a sports event the student is involved in.

- Have lunch with the student.

- Bring books or other materials to the student that are of special interest.

- If appropriate, visit the student at his or her place of employment.

Every Individualized Behavior Plan you develop should contain a specific relationship-building goal that you are committed to meeting.

Introducing an Individualized Classroom Plan to a Student

Once you've developed an Individualized Classroom Plan for a student you need to meet in a one-to-one conference. You have to explain to the student why you are using this plan, what you expect of the student and what the student can expect from you.

Follow these guidelines:

Meet with the student one-to-one.

You need the student's undivided attention, and the student needs to know he or she has yours.

Explain the plan in a caring, empathetic manner.

Emphasize first that you are taking this step to help the student be more successful in the classroom. Do not take a punitive stance. At all times keep the positive relationship in mind as you speak. It's still the most important tool you have for building the student's self-esteem and desire to make changes.

- **Explain the behavior you need.**

  The student needs to clearly understand the specific behaviors you are focusing on. Don't confuse the situation by bringing up behaviors that are not going to be part of this plan.

- **Explain what the student will earn when he or she behaves appropriately.**

  Explain what you are going to do to help him or her choose appropriate behavior. Explain to the student what kinds of positive recognition and support can be earned and how it can be earned. If necessary, to make sure the plan is understood, have the student repeat to you how the incentive system will work. If appropriate, you may want to ask the student what incentive he or she would like to earn.

- **Discuss what will happen if the student does not behave appropriately.**

  Carefully explain the corrective action, or consequence, the student will choose to receive if he or she continues to choose inappropriate behavior. Emphasize that you are not doing this to punish the student but to help him or her. Make sure the student understands that the consequence will be given *each and every time he or she misbehaves.* (And make sure you stick to this promise, too.)

The student needs to clearly understand that under the terms of this plan there will be no warnings and no series of lesser consequences. Each misbehavior will earn the consequence.

- **Review the entire plan. Emphasize that you will be there to help the student.**

   Before the student leaves the meeting be very sure that he or she understands exactly how the individualized plan will work. Encourage him or her to ask questions. Above all, try to make sure that the student leaves the meeting feeling hopeful and confident, not punished or put down. You are giving the student more structure, which he or she needs, but the positive relationship is still your key to eventual success.

Document the meeting.

Be sure to document your meeting. Note the terms of the plan, and how the concept was received by the student. In most cases it is appropriate to share with the parents or the administrator the new individualized plan you have for the student.

Evaluate Your Classroom Plan

One reason many individualized plans, or behavior contracts, are ineffective is that they are carried on for too long a time period. Keep in mind that this is a short-term effort. Your goal is for the student to be able to return to your general classroom management plan as soon as possible.

Plan to use the individualized plan with your student for one to two weeks. At the end of this time, evaluate the student's progress.

Ask yourself:

> Has the student's behavior consistently improved?

If yes, do the following:

• Don't suddenly stop using the plan. Instead, gradually begin phasing out the positive motivation system you are using. Decrease the number of positives earned in a specific time period or increase the time needed to earn the reward.

For example:

- If a student is earning a sticker every 30 minutes, start giving a sticker every 60 minutes instead.

- If a student is able to earn a reward in 3 days, have him or her earn the reward in 5 days.

• Always explain any changes you make to the student. The student needs to understand that he or she is behaving much more responsibly and therefore does not need such frequent reinforcements.

> "Elliot, you've remained in your seat during class for the past two days. Your behavior shows that you're becoming much more responsible in choosing behavior. So we're going to try something a little different. For the next three days I will give you a point every *hour* that you behave instead of every half hour. When you earn 20 points, you will receive a certificate for another book. That should take you about four days. How does that sound?"

• While phasing out the plan, keep the consequences in force.

If you have a general classroom discipline plan in place (as described on page 127), your goal is for the student to return to this plan as quickly as possible. Be sure the student knows exactly when the terms of the individualized plan end and when he or she is once again responsible to the same behavior management plan that you have for all your students. This would be a good time to review the classwide plan with the student, too.

If the student's behavior has not improved with the Individualized Classroom Plan, you can choose to either keep the plan in force a bit longer (you may wish to make adjustments to it) or try something different (see the Individualized Plans that follow.) Use your judgement and knowledge of the student in deciding which course of action will be most beneficial to the student.

Individualized Behavior Plan
Part Two: Home-School Plans

Teachers sometimes find that a Home-School Plan that focuses on parental follow-through at home rather than teacher follow-through at school is an effective strategy to use with difficult students.

A Home-School Plan consists of the following:

1. **Specific behavior** you expect of the student
2. **Positive support** parents will give the student for choosing appropriate behavior at school
3. **Corrective action** parents will take each time the student chooses inappropriate behavior at school

A Home-School Plan is a collaborative effort between you and parents. Its success depends entirely upon a parent's willingness to follow through consistently at home. For that reason, it is important that parents be approached in a positive, confident and concerned manner.

Teachers sometimes report that working with parents of difficult students is often tougher than working with the students themselves. This may be due to a number of reasons:

- The parent's own negative school experiences.

- The parent's personal emotional problems.

- The parent's lack of parenting skills.

- The teacher's inadequate training in how to work effectively with the parents of difficult students.

You can't change a parent's previous experiences, but you can improve his or her perception of you and what *you* stand for. That's why it's so important to be proactive in building a positive relationship with parents as well as with students—right from the start of the school year. For example, if you contact the parent of a difficult student at the beginning of the year (before problems arise) and express your concern and confidence, that parent will be much more likely to be supportive when you call later asking for help.

Positive contact with parents of difficult students must be an ongoing goal. When you need them, you're going to want parents firmly on your side.

Follow these steps when involving parents in a Home-School Plan.

1. Be prepared before you speak with the parent.

Have a clear plan of action in mind before you meet with a parent. Be prepared to discuss the following:

- The specific behaviors you expect of the student (Use the student's behavior profile.)

- The steps you have already taken to help the student choose more appropriate behavior

- Suggested positives and consequences the parent can use at home

- The way you will communicate the student's behavior to the parent

2. Next, meet with the parent.

A one-to-one meeting is the best way to introduce a Home-School Plan to a parent. Here are the points to cover in the meeting.

- **Begin with a statement of concern.**

Always begin a conversation with a parent by expressing your concern and caring for their child. Keep in mind that these are parents who are accustomed to hearing bad news about their child. Hearing a different message from you can have a powerful effect in terms of enlisting their cooperation and support.

> "Mrs. Johnson, let me begin our meeting by first saying that I care about Kenny. He's a great kid and I care that he succeeds in this class. Kenny has the potential to do well, and I'd like to see that happen. That's why I wanted to talk with you today."

- **Describe the specific inappropriate behavior the student engages in.**

Tell the parent the exact behaviors you have observed the child engage in. Avoid value judgements such as "Your child is so difficult," or "She is always causing problems in class." Comments like these give no real information to the parent and can easily trigger defensive, angry responses. Be specific. Explain exactly how the student is noncompliant, and have documentation with you to use if necessary. (The student's behavior profile can be helpful in this situation.)

> "As you can see from these records, Kenny has been talking out in class and pushing and shoving other students. As I've noted here, these problems typically arise when Kenny is working in a group situation, and we do a lot of work in groups. His behavior is a real problem not only for the rest of the class but it's especially a problem for Kenny himself. He's not completing assignments and as a result he's falling far behind in his classwork."

- **Tell the parent the steps you have already taken to handle the problem.**

The parent will want to know that you have already taken steps to help the child. Be sure to explain to the parent exactly what you have done to attempt to solve the problem on your own. Again, have documentation with you.

> "I have met with Kenny several times to discuss these problems. I have clearly explained the appropriate behavior he needs to choose in my class. On the occasions that he has behaved, I have reinforced that behavior. He's earned extra computer time which, as you know, is something he really loves. But it just wasn't enough. He earned computer time twice then fell back into the old habits. As you are aware, Kenny has also been staying after school on a rather consistent basis. None of these things seem to matter enough to him, though."

- **Ask for parental input.**

Find out how the parent feels about the situation. He or she may offer valuable insight that can help you come up with a solution.

> "Is there anything you can tell me that might help me with Kenny?"

- **Let the parent know that you have a plan of action.**

These parents are probably tired of hearing teachers say, "I just don't know what to do with your child." They are often overwhelmed themselves and need the help and support of a strong teacher. They are often desperate for suggestions about what to do to help their child. Your confidence in presenting solutions will increase their own confidence in their ability to help their child.

> "Now that I've explained the problem, let's work on a solution—and there *is* a solution. Over the years I've worked with many students like Kenny, and I have a plan for how we can help him."

- **Emphasize that you cannot do it on your own—that you must have parental help.**

Parents may not believe that they have much influence over their child, but most children do care what their parents think about them. It is extremely important, therefore, to emphasize to parents that they are the most important people in their child's life and that they need to use their influence to help their child. Explain that only by working together will you have the best chance for helping the child succeed.

> "The success of this plan depends on both of us working together. I'm Kenny's teacher, and I'll do as much as I can to help him, but you're his parent—you're the most important person in his life. You have an influence with Kenny that's far more powerful than mine. I need *your* help if we are to help Kenny."

- **Introduce the concept of a Home-School Plan and clarify the actions the parent will take at home in response to the student's behavior.**

Introduce the concept of the Home-School Plan to the parent. Explain the role you would like the parent to play—to positively reinforce the student on days when he or she behaves, and to provide a consequence on days the student does not behave. Talk about appropriate positives and consequences. Parents often have no idea what constitutes an effective reward or corrective action.

Explain that the student does not always need to earn a "prize" each day, but rather can earn points toward a reward. ("Each day you bring home a positive report from your teacher you will earn a point. When you have earned five points you may have a friend sleep over.") Consequences, however, must be provided each day that a negative report comes home.

Your suggestions should reflect the student's age and your own knowledge of the student's needs. Before the meeting ends, you will want to agree upon both the positive recognition and consequences the parent will provide each day.

> "I'd like to try something with Kenny that I call a Home-School Plan. With this plan we're going to focus our attention on Kenny's biggest problem behaviors: talking out in class and pushing and shoving. Each day Kenny behaves appropriately, no talking out, no pushing or shoving, I'll let you know and you will reward him at home for his good behavior. Each day he does not behave appropriately you will follow through at home with a consequence—something he doesn't like. Now, what do you think Kenny would like to earn as a reward? (*Teacher and parent discuss ideas and agree on the reward.*) What would be a good consequence to give him if he misbehaves? (*Teacher and parent discuss ideas and agree on the consequence.*)"

- **Tell the parent that you will send home a note each day.**

Tell the parent that each day you will send a note home to let him or her know how the student behaved that day. A positive report means the student will receive the predetermined reward from the parent. A negative report means that the parent will provide the prearranged consequence.

Reiterate that it is absolutely vital that the parent be consistent in following through. If the student feels the plan will be enforced only sporadically it will lose all effectiveness.

"Every day I'll send a note home with Kenny letting you know how he behaved that day. If he behaved appropriately, you will follow through with the reward we've agreed on. If the note tells you that Kenny didn't behave, you will follow through with the consequence. Now I know that it's easy to give your child a reward and very hard to follow through with something he doesn't like, but it is very important that Kenny understands that each negative report from school means a consequence at home. He has to understand that we're not kidding. That you and I are working together. And that we mean business."

- **Explain the Home-School Plan to the student.**

At this point in your conversation you may want to ask the student to join you. With parent and teacher presenting a united front, explain the Home-School Plan to the student. The student may be angry. He or she may brush the whole thing off. No matter how the student responds, make it very clear that you and the parent are working together for his or her benefit—and that you both are ready to do what it takes to help the student succeed.

> Keep in mind the communication skills we have addressed in this book, and don't let yourself, or the parent, get dragged into an argument with the student. If you find the parent becoming involved in such an argument with the student, try to mediate and keep the conversation focused on the plan. It is important that the student leaves the meeting feeling he has positive support, not negative pressure.

On the following pages are sample Home-School Plans for students who need attention, students who need limits and students who need motivation.

Use these samples as a reference for putting together your own individualized Home-School Plan.

Home-School Plan for a Student Who Needs Attention
Elementary

Behaviors

- You will not talk without permission.

- You will stay in your seat.

Positive Support

- Each day a note will be sent home to your parents.

- If you have not been disruptive that day, as indicated on the note, your parent(s) will spend an extra 15 minutes with you in an activity of your choice.

Corrective Action

- If you have continued to shout and get out of your seat and run around the classroom, you will lose the right to watch TV that night.

This Home-School Contract recognizes the needs of this attention-seeking student. The reward the student will earn (suggested and agreed upon by the parent) is time spent with the parent—a meaningful goal to this student. And in this case the consequence is loss of television privileges, something the parent knows this student doesn't want to lose.

Home-School Plan for a Student
Who Needs Attention
Middle/Secondary

Behaviors

- You will not talk without permission.

- You will stay in your seat.

Positive Support

- Each day a note will be sent home to your parents.

- For each day that you have behaved appropriately, you will receive a point. When you have earned 5 points, you will be allowed to stay out later on the weekend with your friends.

Corrective Action

- If you have engaged in inappropriate behavior, the note will indicate such and you will be grounded for one night on the weekend.

Home-School Plan for a Student Who Needs Limits
Elementary

Behaviors

- You will follow directions; you will not argue.

- You will not argue or fight with other students.

Positive Support

- You will be given a note to take home each day.

- For each day that you behave appropriately, your parents will give you a point. When you have received 5 points you will be allowed to select a video at the video store.

Corrective Action

- Each day that you are disruptive, your parents will take away a privilege, such as watching TV or using the telephone that evening.

Home-School Plan for a Student Who Needs Limits
Middle/Secondary

Behaviors

- You will follow directions; you will not argue.

- You will not argue or fight with other students.

Positive Support

- Each day that you behave, a note will be sent home to your parents.

- When you have received 10 notes you will be allowed to purchase a CD of your choice.

Corrective Action

- If you talk back and refuse to work, your parent will be called.

- Your parent will come to school and spend the day with you. (See pages 239-247 for an explanation of this technique.)

Home-School Plan for a Student Who Needs Motivation
Elementary

Behaviors

- You will complete assignments.

- You will participate in class activities.

Positive Support

- Each day, a student from an upper-level class will be available to tutor you for one-half hour.

- Each day that your work is complete, it will be sent home.

- For each assignment you complete, your parents will give you a point. When you have earned 10 points, you will be able to rent a video game.

Corrective Action

- You will finish all incomplete assignments at home. Until homework is completed, the phone and television are off limits.

Home-School Plan for a Student Who Needs Motivation
Middle/Secondary

Behaviors

- You will complete all assignments.

- You will participate in class activities.

Positive Support

- Two days a week you will have a peer tutor available to you.

- Each day that your assignments are complete, you will earn a point. When you have earned 5 points, you will earn the right to purchase a tape.

Corrective Action

- If your work is not completed, you will be grounded at home until the work is finished.

Call the parent to evaluate the effectiveness of the Home-School Plan.

Once the Home-School Plan is in effect, stay in close touch with the parent. Phone calls home will not only let you know how things are going, but your own inquiries will also serve to motivate the parent to be consistent in following through with positives and consequences. Consistency in discipline is difficult for most parents. Your interest and support may be a very appreciated lifeline to a frustrated parent.

Like an Individual Classroom Plan, the Home-School Plan should also be in effect for only one or two weeks. At the end of this time, evaluate its effectiveness.

Ask yourself, "Has the student's behavior improved to an acceptable level?"

If yes, call the parent and agree upon a plan of action for fading out the contract.

For example:

> Tell the parent that instead of sending a note home every day, you will send a note every other day.

Be sure the student is informed of any changes you and the parent make in the plan and clarify to parents that consequences remain in effect until the student returns to the general classroom plan.

If the student's behavior has not improved, you can choose to either keep the plan in force a while longer (you and the parent may wish to make adjustments to it) or turn to additional strategies. Use your judgement, and knowledge of the student and parent, in deciding which course of action will be most beneficial to the student.

Continue to Build the Positive Relationship

As with a Classroom Plan, you need to continue to set relationship-building goals for yourself. To further enhance the home-school partnership that you are encouraging, your goals can be tied to positive communication that reaches both student and parent.

For example:

- Positive phone calls to parent at home
- Positive phone calls to student
- Positive notes home
- If appropriate, a positive home visit

Individualized Behavior Plans
Part Three—Administrator Plans

An administrator's role in dealing with difficult students usually involves providing consequences for misbehavior. A trip to the office typically means that a student is in trouble. The administrator, however, can offer a great deal more. He or she can be a potent force in building the difficult student's trust in school.

The involvement of your administrator (or other support staff) in an Individualized Behavior Plan can have a powerful impact on a difficult student. Your administrator may not only be able to provide stronger, more effective consequences, but, more importantly, he or she can also provide unique motivation and help to develop a positive relationship with this student.

An Administrator Plan consists of the following:

> 1. **Specific behaviors** you expect of the student
>
> 2. **Positive support** the administrator will give the student for choosing appropriate behavior
>
> 3. **Corrective action** the administrator will take each time the student chooses inappropriate behavior

The Administrator Plan should also include relationship-building goals that the administrator is committed to fulfilling.

Here's how administrator involvement can benefit the needs of different students:

 Students Who Need Attention

You know that these students want attention from you and from peers. But they may *really* be motivated to behave if they have an opportunity to receive special recognition from the principal. Rewards such as lunch with the principal or a special certificate or personal note of congratulations can have great impact on a student who, above all, craves and needs attention.

 Students Who Need Limits

What is often overlooked with power students is the fact that though they may not want attention or support from you, they may like the support or positive reinforcement they receive from the administrator or other support staff at school. ("I'm going to deal with the top guy!")

An Individualized Behavior Plan that includes recognition from an administrator may motivate this student where your own recognition did not.

Likewise, firmer corrective actions such as in-school suspension and conferencing with parents can also be provided through the administrator.

 ## Students Who Need Motivation

There are some unmotivated students who just will not work for you. But they may be motivated by the recognition and reinforcement of the administrator or other support staff at school. One effective way to involve the administrator is to ask him or her to help the student get started on assignments.

The administrator can also be involved in holding the student accountable for completing work. Some administrators have students stay in their office after school to complete assignments. Others establish study halls where students need to go to complete work they have not completed in class. These special study halls are monitored closely by an adult, and students are expected to complete their work there.

On the following pages you will find sample Administrator Plans for students who need attention, students who need limits and students who need motivation.

Use these samples as a reference for developing an Individualized Behavior Plan with an administrator or other support staff. Note that the positives and consequences used are appropriate to the students' needs.

Note also that each plan includes a suggested relationship-building goal for the administrator.

Administrator Plan for a Student Who Needs Attention
Elementary

Behaviors
- You will not talk without permission.
- You will stay in your seat.

Positive Support
- For every 15 minutes you spend without talking out or running around the room, you will receive a stamp on your tracking chart.
- When your tracking chart is filled, you will earn the right to be the principal's assistant for two hours.

Corrective Action
- If you continue to talk and get out of your seat and run around the classroom, you will sit by yourself in the principal's office for 45 minutes to calm down.

Relationship Building
- The administrator has lunch with the student.

Administrator Plan for a
Student Who Needs Attention
Middle/Secondary

Behaviors

- You will not talk without permission.

- You will stay in your seat.

Positive Support

- For each day that you behave appropriately during the entire period, you will receive a point. When you have earned 10 points you may choose to have lunch with the vice principal, principal or counselor.

Corrective Action

- Every time you continue to disrupt in class you will spend the remainder of the day in in-school suspension.

Relationship Building

- The administrator goes to an event in which the student is participating.

Administrator Plan for a
Student Who Needs Limits
Elementary

Behaviors
- You will follow directions; you will not argue.
- You will not argue or fight with other students.

Positive Support
- For each 30-minute period you spend following directions without arguing, you will earn a point.
- When you have received 15 points you will go to the principal's office to receive the principal's award.

Corrective Action
- Whenever you refuse to follow directions, argue or fight, you will be sent to in-school suspension for one hour.

Relationship Building
- Administrator will come to class each day and spend five minutes in class helping the student.

Administrator Plan for a Student Who Needs Limits
Middle/Secondary

Behaviors

- You will follow directions; you will not argue.

- You will not argue or fight with other students.

Positive Support

- For each day (period) you behave appropriately, you will receive a point.

- When you have received 10 points, the vice principal will give you a gift certificate from a local merchant.

Corrective Action

- Each time you talk back and refuse to work, you will spend the rest of the day in in-school suspension.

Relationship Building

- Administrator will meet one-to-one with the student on a regular basis, as will the homeroom teacher.

Administrator Plan for a
Student Who Needs Motivation
Elementary

Behaviors

- You will complete assignments.

- You will participate in class activities.

Positive Support

- Each day that you complete your work, you will go to the principal's office and select a prize from the principal's surprise box.

- Each day, a student from an upper-level class will be available to tutor you for one-half hour.

Corrective Action

- If you have not completed your work during class, you will stay after school in the principal's office until work is completed at which time your parent will be called to pick you up.

Relationship Building

- The administrator will spend time with the student.

Administrator Plan for a
Student Who Needs Motivation
Middle/Secondary

Behaviors

- You will complete assignments.

- You will participate in class activities.

Positive Support

- Twice a week you will have a peer tutor for one period.

- For each assignment that you complete, you will receive a point. When you have earned 10 points, you may go to the administrator's office to receive a gift certificate.

Corrective Action

- If you have not completed your work, you will be assigned detention before school, at lunch or after school in order to complete your work.

Relationship Building

- The administrator will spend time with the student.

Meet with your administrator.

Follow these guidelines if you feel that an individualized Administrator Plan would benefit a particular difficult student:

Meet with the administrator to discuss the plan.

- Let the principal know the steps you have already taken with the student. Explain that at this point you need stronger, more structured intervention and you feel he or she can offer a unique contribution that just might make a difference with this student.

Explain how you would like the administrator to help.

- Have a plan of action in mind before you meet with the administrator. By this point you know your student well. Use that knowledge, and the information presented in this chapter, to put together a plan that is designed to meet the student's specific needs. The administrator, of course, can make changes or offer different suggestions, but you will have a working framework from which to proceed.

Emphasize the contribution that can be made if the administrator commits to relationship-building goals with this student.

- Explain all that you are doing to build a positive relationship with this student. Talk about your successes and the positive changes you have seen. When you ask the administrator to be a part of this relationship-building process have specific ideas in mind that are geared to meeting this student's needs (see suggestions on the sample plans pages 232-237).

Once a plan is agreed upon, meet with the student.

- Follow the guidelines for presenting an Individualized Classroom Plan to a student (pages 211-213). Depending on the situation, the administrator can meet alone with the student or you also can be present.

Evaluate the plan.

Like any Individualized Behavior Plan, this one must be evaluated carefully and often. If the student's behavior improves you will want to phase out the plan gradually. If no improvement is seen, you and the administrator may choose to make adjustments.

Administrator/Teacher/Parent Empowerment Conference

Sometimes it is necessary for all the significant people in a difficult student's life to get together and work as a team to help him or her make behavioral changes. On his or her own, an administrator, teacher or parent may not always be able to influence the student to choose more responsible behavior. Working together, however, each can be more empowered to play an active, effective role in making a difference with the student.

Such a team effort can be especially beneficial to a parent who has been ineffective in following through at home. The coordinated efforts of a team can give the parent the confidence and support to take steps he or she might not otherwise have taken.

One highly effective approach to involving the parents of an extremely difficult student is to meet together and set up the following contingency within a Home-School Plan:

> When a student continues to misbehave, the administrator will request the parent come to school and spend the day—all day—in class with the student.

We've rarely seen a more powerful way to get a difficult student on the right track. The parent sees exactly how the student behaves in school, and the student feels pressure from peers about the parent being in school. Often all it takes is one day of the parent coming to school to make a dramatic impact on the student.

In the scenario that follows, the parent, perhaps for the first time ever, is motivated to take a proactive stance in dealing with her child. The support of the administrator and teacher give her the confidence to make that commitment. Knowing that she had found it difficult to follow through at home, they also give her a concrete suggestion that she is willing to follow through on.

Administrator: Good afternoon, Mrs. Smith. Mr. Collins and I really appreciate your coming in today.

Mrs. Smith: Yeah, it's hard to come in. You know, I had to take time off from work. This isn't easy.

Teacher: We understand it's not easy, and we wouldn't ask you to come in if it weren't important, but this is the situation: I'm really concerned about your daughter. I'm concerned about Laura's success in school. We have some problems with her that we really need to work on. Let me explain what's going on. Laura continues to talk back to me. And she continues to refuse to do her work. I've tried a number of things with her. I've spoken with her. I have set up a behavior contract with her. I've sent her to another classroom for misbehavior. And I've met with her many times one-on-one, trying to get through to her, trying to help her understand that her behavior is hurting her. Nothing has helped, and I'm very concerned about her.

Mrs. Smith: Well, that makes two of us, because I've just about had it, too. I can't do much more than I am doing. It's tough being a single mom. It's tough going to work every day and still trying to look after children. I get home late. I'm exhausted. Like I said, I had to leave work early to come here today. I don't know what else I can do. I'm doing as much as I can. Really, I've had it.

Administrator: Well, let's look at it this way, then. Laura doesn't listen to you, and she doesn't listen to her teacher. But who is she hurting? Herself. Laura's the one who's going to be the big loser if something doesn't change. The answer is for all of us to team up to work together to help her.

Mrs. Smith: Like how?

Teacher: Well, you and I have tried a few things already, like having you follow through at home by grounding and taking away privileges. But none of that really worked, did it?

Mrs. Smith: I guess not. I get home so late that I don't know if she's stayed grounded or not. It's hard to follow through when I'm not around. I do the best I can, but it's hard.

Administrator: We know you're doing the best you can. And we know it's hard raising kids by yourself. And I have seen how upset your daughter can get. She can get pretty intimidating when she yells and screams.

Mrs. Smith: Yeah, just like her father talking to me. It's unbelievable.

Administrator: Her father isn't the issue. Our concern is Laura, and what we can do to help her. I've worked with a lot of kids like Laura before and believe me, there are answers. But those answers lie in our working together. You know, you really are the most important person in Laura's life. To turn things around for Laura, we all have to be a team. You have a lot more influence over her than I do or Mr. Collins does.

Mrs. Smith: You know, that's interesting because I feel like her friends are the most important people in her life.

Teacher: Believe me, you are. That's why we need to work together. Do you know what we have to show Laura? That we're not going away. We need to show Laura that she cannot intimidate us like she has other teachers. Like she's intimidated you. I have an idea that might be just what we need. Now, nothing has worked very well so far, has it?

Mrs. Smith: No.

Administrator: Okay. Here's something that is often very effective with students Laura's age. If Laura chooses to misbehave and not do her work, then you, her mom, will come to school and spend the day with her.

Mrs. Smith: What? Come to school? I'd have to take another day off. What would I do at school? I don't get it. What's the point? Really, I can't take any more time off from work.

Teacher: If Laura had a 104-degree temperature would you take a day off from work?

Mrs. Smith: Well, that's different. Of course I would if she were really sick.

Administrator: It's not different at all. Mrs. Smith, we're really worried about Laura's success at school. We're worried that she just isn't going to make it. And the truth is, Laura won't make it in school unless we all work together. It may take her seeing you sitting there beside her, all day long, to understand that we are a team, that we mean business, that we are not going to be intimidated and that we're going to work with her so she will succeed.

Mrs. Smith: You really think it will make a difference if I come to school? If I can arrange the time off do you think that will do it?

Teacher: It's a good start, and it's part of the process, but that alone is not the answer. I'm going to continue to work with Laura. I'm going to continue building a positive relationship with her. I'm going to give her a lot of support and continue working with her on the academic difficulties she has. But to answer your question, your coming to school might be a step in the right direction.

Mrs. Smith: Okay, then I'm willing to try. At least once.

Administrator: Good. Now I know that when we present this idea to Laura she's not going to be too excited about it.

Mrs. Smith: Hardly. I think she'll just about die of embarrassment if I show up at school.

Administrator: That's right, she probably will. But the point is, Mrs. Smith, it's Laura's choice whether or not you come. If she chooses to do her work—if she chooses to not talk back—this will never happen. It's Laura's choice completely.

Laura's sitting outside now. I think we should talk to her together.

Mrs. Smith: Okay, let's do it.

Teacher: Just follow our lead. We'll let Laura know that we're all a team.

Mrs. Smith: I'm ready.

Laura comes into the conference.

Administrator: Laura, we wanted you to come in because your mom, Mr. Collins and I are concerned about you and your behavior at school. We've been talking, and we've put together a plan to help you be more successful at school. Laura, we know that you feel everyone's against you, but the truth is we all care about you and we need to help you make better choices. We cannot have you talking back in class anymore. You're going to have to do your work. That's all there is to it. Do you have anything you'd like to say?

Laura: I don't have to do it just 'cause you say so.

Mrs. Smith: I can't believe you're doing at school what you do at home. I am so ashamed of you.

Laura: How would you know what I do at home? You're never there, Mom.

Mrs. Smith: Laura, I can't believe you're acting like this here in front of your teacher and your principal. I've tried my best to give you what you need.

Teacher: Okay, now here's the issue, Laura. Your mom and Mrs. Brooks and I are working together. We want to help you, and we're not going away. We've got a plan to help you make better choices at school and here's what it comes down to: If you choose to talk back to me in class, if you refuse to do what I tell you to do, if you choose to be disruptive in class, you're going to choose to have your mom come to school to spend the entire day with you.

Laura:	You know you won't take time off of work, Mom. You won't do that.
Mrs. Smith:	Laura, I'm going to do it.
Laura:	No way.
Mrs. Smith:	Yes, I am going to do it.
Laura:	Maybe to be with your boyfriend, Robert, you'd take time off from work.
Mrs. Smith:	You know you're getting to be just like your father and I've really had it, Laura.
Administrator:	(*defusing a potential confrontation*) Okay, Laura, the issue is this. Your mom will come to school. It's your choice. She'll come as many times as it takes for you to recognize that you have to make better choices.
Laura:	And what's she going to do there?
Teacher:	She will spend the entire day with you, sitting right next to you.
Laura:	Like right in the classroom? No way.
Teacher:	That's exactly right. Right in the classroom.
Mrs. Smith:	I'm going to come to your class, Laura, and if you don't change your attitude right now you'll sure be changing it when we get home today.
Administrator:	Now wait. Mrs. Smith, I want to be very clear about something. I hear you're upset with Laura, but please understand that we are not talking about corporal punishment—that may not be the answer at all. Remember, Laura's consequence is that you will come to school.

Mrs. Smith: Okay. And I've agreed. I will come to school, Laura, and you'd better believe it.

Laura: You're not going to be sitting next to me in my classes.

Mrs. Smith: You're going to be surprised.

Administrator: Whose choice is it, Laura, whether or not your mom comes to school and sits next to you?

Laura: Yeah, all right. Okay. I hear you.

Mrs. Smith: You'd better believe it, Laura, because it's going to happen and this is because I do care about you.

Teacher: I know you may feel we don't care, Laura, but we're doing this precisely because we all care about what happens to you.

Laura: She cares about Robert. That's all she cares about. She doesn't know what I do. She doesn't know what I feel.

Mrs. Smith: Let me in, Laura. Just let me in. I do care, and I'm going to show you by coming to school if I have to.

Teacher: Laura, you're not alone in working things out here at school. We're here to help you. It's your choice, but we're going to be right here to help. We're not going away.

Laura: Yeah, you're not going away, all right. You'll be ganging up on me all the time. I can see that.

Teacher: We're not doing this to gang up on you. We're doing this to give you some structure to help you.

Laura: Yeah, right.

The student needed more help from this parent—help that the parent did not know how to give on her own. Through guidance from the administrator and teacher, this parent now sees herself as empowered. She now knows she's not alone. Likewise, the administrator and teacher have an ally who will give them support when they need it. In addition, the student has learned that the parent, administrator and teacher are a team; she can no longer play one against the other.

Summary

When you are working with students who require an Individualized Behavior Plan, there are often no simple answers. Some individualized plans may work for awhile. Then, in spite of everything you've done, you might find the student falling back into disruptive behavior patterns.

There is no magical answer that will solve all the student's behavior problems at once. With difficult students change happens slowly.

Every baby step forward may be hard earned. Every step backward must be viewed not as failure but as a challenge to try something new.

With difficult students you need to be willing to consistently evaluate, restructure, and follow through on your behavior management efforts. Most of all, however, you must continue to build a positive relationship with the student.

We have never met a teacher who was truly successful with a difficult student who did not first gain the student's trust.

CONCLUSION

Underlying everything, our message in this book is this: With difficult students you do have a choice. No matter what negative experiences you may have had in the past, and in spite of the difficulties these students may present to you now, you can make the choice to take control and make a difference in the future.

You can choose to take the steps that will help your difficult students succeed *and* that will make teaching more satisfying for you.

In this book we have presented a variety of techniques and procedures that teachers use to help difficult students reach their potential. It is our hope that after gaining an understanding of all the skills presented, you will then use your own professional judgement, and your knowledge of your students, to decide how to best use these skills. Keep in mind that in dealing with difficult students there is no absolute, sequential approach that is going to be effective all of the time.

Working with difficult students is like riding a roller coaster. There will be ups, and, just as surely, there will be downs. You will need to respond to these ups and downs by evaluating, reassessing and trying different approaches as needed.

Too often we feel that once students improve their behavior they should be able to sustain that improvement. We expect that if we've taught behavior, provided positive support and, if necessary, used an Individualized Behavior Plan, any success the student experiences should be ongoing.

We're usually not prepared for the roller coaster to dip down, and after a few such disheartening dips, we often give up.

Succeeding with difficult students takes perseverance and patience.

Above all, it takes a willingness to consistently communicate to the student that you care and are not going away. You'll be there for the ups and you'll stick with the student during the downs. You are prepared to do whatever is needed to help the student succeed.

This is a message that many students have never heard before. When a difficult student realizes that a caring adult has made such a significant commitment, he or she may work to begin changing behavior and *you* will find yourself succeeding with difficult students.

RECOMMENDED READING AND BIBLIOGRAPHY

Albert, L. *Cooperative Discipline*. Circle Pines, Minnesota: American Guidance Service, 1991.

Atkeson, B. M., and Forehand, R. "Home-based Reinforcement Programs Designed to Modify Classroom Behavior: A Review and Methodological Evaluation," *Psychological Bulletin*, 86(6), pp.1298-1308, 1979.

Brophy, J., and Evertson, C. *Learning From Teaching: A Developmental Perspective*. Boston: Allyn and Bacon, 1976.

Chalfant, J. C., Pysh, M. and Moultrie, R. "Teacher Assistance Teams: A Model for Within-building Problem Solving," *Learning Disabilities Quarterly*, 2, pp. 85-96, 1979.

Charles, C. M. *Building Classroom Discipline*. New York: Longman, 1989.

Cullinan, D., and Epstein, M. H. "Behavior Disorders." *Exceptional Children and Youth* 4th ed., ed. N. Haring. Columbus, Ohio: Merrill, 1986.

Davidson, H., and Lang, G. "Children's Perceptions of Their Teacher's Feelings Towards Them." *Journal of Experimental Education*, 29, pp. 109-118, 1960.

Dinkmeyer, D. *Systematic Training For Effective Teaching*. Circle Pines, Minnesota: American Guidance Service, 1979.

Dolliver, P., Lewis, A. F., and McLaughlin, T. F. "Effects of a Daily Report Card on Academic Performance and Classroom Behavior." *Remedial and Special Education*, 6(1), pp. 51-52, 1985.

Doyle, W. *Classroom Management*. West Lafayette, Indiana: Kappa Delta Phi, 1980.

Dreikurs, and Cassel, P. *Discipline Without Tears*. New York: Hawthorn, 1972.

Dreikurs, R. Grunwald. *Maintaining Sanity in the Classroom*. New York: Harper and Row, 1971.

Englander, M. *Strategies For Classroom Discipline*. New York: Praeger, 1986.

Evans, J. H., Bostow, D. E., Geiger, G., and Drash, P. W. "Increasing Assignment Completion and Accuracy Using a Daily Report Card Procedure." *Psychology in the Schools*, 19, pp. 540-547, 1982.

Evertson, et al. *Classroom Management for Elementary Teachers*. Englewood Cliffs, New Jersey: Prentice Hall, 1984.

Glasser, W., "Ten Steps To Good Discipline." *Today's Education*, 66, pp. 61-63, 1977.

Good, T., and Brophy, J. *Looking Into Classrooms*. 2nd ed. New York: Harper and Row, 1978.

Gordon, T. *Teacher Effectiveness Training*. New York: Wyden, 1984.

Gresham, F. M. "Use of a Home-based Dependent Group Contingency System in Controlling Destructive Behavior: A Case Study," *School Psychology Review*, 12(2), pp. 195-199, 1983.

Imber, S. C., Imber, R. B., and Rothstein, C. "Modifying Independent Work Habits: An Effective Teacher-Parent Communication Program," *Exceptional Children*, 45, pp. 218-221, 1979.

Jones, F., *Positive Classroom Discipline*. New York: McGraw Hill, 1987.

Kauffman, J. M. *Characteristics of Children's Behavior Disorders*. 3rd ed. Columbus, Ohio: Merrill, 1985.

Kelley, T. J., Bullock, C. M., and Dykes, M. K. "Behavior Disorders: Teachers Perceptions." *Exceptional Children*, 43, pp. 316-18, 1977.

Long, N. J., and Newman, R. G., "Managing Surface Behavior of Children in School, " *Conflict in the Classroom: The Education of Emotionally Disturbed Children*. 4th ed. Belmount, California: Wadsworth, 1980.

Lovitt, T. C. "Self-management Projects with Children with Behavior Disabilities," *Journal of Learning Disabilities*, 6, pp. 138-150, 1973.

Madsen, C., Becker, W., and Thomas, D. "Rules, Praise and Ignoring: Elements of Elementary Classroom Control," *Journal of Applied Behavioral Analysis*, 1, pp. 139-150, 1968.

Mc Laughlin, T., and Malaby, J. "Reducing and Measuring Inappropriate Verbalizations in a Token Economy," *Journal of Applied Behavioral Analysis*, pp. 329-333, 1972.

McGinnis, E., and Goldstein, A. P. *Skillstreaming the Elementary School Child*. Champaign, Illinois: Research Press Company, 1984.

Morgan, D., and Jenson, W. *Teaching Behaviorally Disordered Students*. Columbus: Merrill Publishing Company, 1988.

Morrison, A., and McIntrye, D. *Teachers and Teaching*. Baltimore: Penguin, 1969.

O'Leary, D., and O'Leary, S. eds. *Classroom Management: Successful Use of Behavior Modification*. 2nd ed. New York: Pergamon Press, 1977.

Paine, S. *Structuring Your Classroom for Academic Success*. Champaign, Illinois: Research Press Company, 1981.

Rosenshine, B. *Enthusiastic Teaching: A Research Review*. School Review, 72, pp. 449-514, 1983.

Schumaker, J. B., Hovell, M. F., and Sherman, J. A. "An Analysis of Daily Report Cards and Parent-Managed Privileges in the Improvement of Adolescents' Classroom Performance," *Journal of Applied Behavior Analysis*, 10, pp. 449-464, 1977.

Stokes, S. ed. *School-based Staff Support Teams: A Blueprint for Action*. Bloomington: Indiana University; National Inservice Network, 1981.

Van Houten, R. *Are Social Reprimands Effective?* and S. Axelrod and J. Apsche eds. The Effects of Punishment on Human Behavior. New York: Academic Press, 1983.

Walker, H. M., and Buckley, K. "Teacher Attention to Appropriate and Inappropriate Classroom Behavior: An Individual Case Study," *Focus On Exceptional Children*, 5, pp. 5-11, 1973.

Walker, H., et al., "Deviant Classroom Behavior as a Function of Combinations of Social and Token Reinforcement and Cost Contingency," *Behavior Therapy*, 7, pp. 76-88, 1976.

White, M. "Natural Rates of Teacher Approval and Disapproval in the Classroom," *Journal of Applied Behavioral Analysis*, 8, pp. 367-372, 1975.

Witt, J. C., Hannafin, M. J. and Martens, B. K. "Home-based Reinforcement: Behavioral Conspiration Between Academic Performance and Inappropriate Behavior," *Journal of School Psychology*, 21, pp. 337-348, 1983.

Wyka, G., Jeliwske, M. S. *The Art of Limit Setting*. Brookfield, Wisconsin: National Crisis Prevention Institute, 1991.

About the Authors

Lee and Marlene Canter are well known for their work in the fields of education and parenting. Together they have developed four nationally recognized professional development programs: Assertive Discipline®, Parents On Your Side®, Homework Without Tears® and Succeeding With Difficult Students™. They have written over 40 books and produced more than 10 video programs geared to helping educators and parents raise happy, responsible children.

Prior to founding Lee Canter and Associates in 1976, Lee Canter pursued a career in social work, working with child guidance agencies throughout California. Marlene Canter began her career as a resource specialist focusing on teaching students with special needs.

Today Lee and Marlene manage Lee Canter and Associates, a company dedicated to researching and developing innovative and effective programs that help educators and parents work together to improve the quality of education for children everywhere.

Over the past 17 years, Lee and Marlene Canter and their staff have trained over 1,000,000 educators and parents. Articles about Lee Canter have appeared in major educational publications as well as in *Newsweek*, *U.S. News & World Report*, the *New York Times* and the *Los Angeles Times*. Lee is frequently a featured speaker at national educational conferences and has made numerous television appearances, including the "Today Show" and "Oprah Winfrey."

Lee and Marlene, both native Californians, reside in Los Angeles with their two children, Josh and Nicole.

Materials for Teachers
from Lee Canter & Associates

BEHAVIOR MANAGEMENT

CA1000	Assertive Discipline Text (revised edition)
CA1001	Assertive Discipline Elementary Workbook, Gr. K–5
CA1003	Assertive Discipline Middle Sch Workbook, Gr. 6–8
CA1005	Assertive Discipline Secondary Workbook, Gr. 9–12
CA1018	Seasonal Motivators
CA1026	Teacher's Mailbox
CA1029	Back to School with Assertive Discipline
CA1033	Desktop Motivators, Gr. 1–4
CA1034	Awards for Reinforcing Positive Behavior, Gr. 1–3
CA1035	Awards for Reinforcing Positive Behavior, Gr. 4–6
CA1042	Bulletin Boards for Reinf. Positive Behav., Gr. K–3
CA1043	Bulletin Boards for Reinf. Positive Behav., Gr. 4–6
CA1048	Positive Reinforcement Activities, Gr. K–6
CA1052	Positive Reinforcement Activities, Gr. 7–12
CA1061	Monthly Citizen Slips
CA1063	Teacher's Plan Book Plus #2
CA1064	Teacher's Plan Book Plus #1
CA2525	Succeeding With Difficult Students Text, Gr. K–12
CA2527	Succeeding With Difficult Students Wkbk, Gr. K–12
CA2529	Behavior Documentation Log **NEW**
CA2707	The High-Performing Teacher Text **NEW**
CA3017	Record Book Plus

PARENT INVOLVEMENT

CA1009	Assertive Discipline for Parents
CA1010	Parent Resource Guide
CA1205	Homework Without Tears–Parent Guide
CA1215	Homework Without Tears–Parent Guide — in Spanish
CA2004	Parents On Your Side text, Gr. K–12
CA2010	Parents On Your Side Workbook, Gr. K–8
CA2033	Teacher's Plan Book Plus #4
CA2053	Managing the Morning Rush **NEW**
CA2054	Winning the Chores Wars **NEW**
CA2055	Help! It's Homework Time **NEW**
CA2056	Couch Potato Kids **NEW**
CA2057	Surviving Sibling Rivalry **NEW**
CA2058	No More Bedtime Battles **NEW**

HOMEWORK AND STUDY SKILLS

CA1217	Teaching Responsible Homework Habits, Gr. 1–3
CA1218	Teaching Responsible Homework Habits, Gr. 4–6
CA1219	Teaching Responsible Homework Habits, Gr. 6–8
CA1223	Homework Organizer for Students, Gr. 4–8
CA1247	How to Write a Research Paper, Gr. 5–8
CA1248	How to Study and Take Tests, Gr. 5–8
CA1249	How to Use the Library, Gr. 5–8
CA1250	How to Write Better Book Reports, Gr. 5–8
CA1260	Teacher's Plan Book Plus #3

For the location of your nearest school supply store or to request a free catalog, contact Lee Canter & Associates.

Teachers: You can earn graduate credits* this semester!

New Course on Violence Prevention – Fall 1994

NEW!

- **The High-Performing Teacher™**
- **Succeeding With Difficult Students®**
- **Assertive Discipline and Beyond®**
- **How To Get Parents On Your Side®**

Enroll today! Experience the most exciting, most rewarding graduate courses on video in the comfort and convenience of your home or school. Weeklong graduate courses are also available at university campuses each summer.

*Earn 3 semester or 5 quarter hours of graduate credit, depending upon the university offering the course in your area.

To find out how you can improve behavior in your classroom, gain parent support, or prevent violence in your school, call this special graduate course number.

Graduate Course Information

800-677-4791

Ask for Charlie.